Civic Center

HOW DID I GET HERE?

HOW DID I GET HERE?

THE ASCENT OF AN UNLIKELY CEO

TONY HAWK
WITH PAT HAWK

WILEY

John Wiley & Sons, Inc.

Published by John Wiley & Sons, Inc., Hoboken, New Jersey.
Published simultaneously in Canada.

For general information on our other products and services or for technical support,
please contact our Customer Care Department within the United States at (800)
762-2974, outside the United States at (317) 572-3993 or fax (317) 572-4002.

Wiley also publishes its books in a variety of electronic formats. Some content that
appears in print may not be available in electronic books. For more information about
Wiley products, visit our web site at www.wiley.com.

ISBN 978-0-470-63149-2 (cloth): ISBN 978-0-470-93019-9 (ebk);
ISBN 978-0-470-93020-5 (ebk); ISBN 978-0-470-93021-2 (ebk)

Printed in the United States of America.

10 9 8 7 6 5 4 3 2 1

31232009106149

CONTENTS

PREFACE

This book would not exist without my sister Pat, who has been my navigator through this uncharted territory of mixing professional skateboarding, licensing, mainstream sponsorship, event planning, film production, and philanthropy. We have learned together, but she has kept the businesses running smoothly when everything else seems to be spinning into chaos.

It's funny: As I began to embrace the idea of doing this book, she started realizing what a daunting project it would become. We complemented each other in that respect, and it is a perfect metaphor for how we work together. I throw the unreal ideas out there, and she makes them reality.

Nobody could have helped more with the actual writing than my brother Steve. He can craft disjointed facts, cryptic time lines, and nonsensical stream-of-consciousness e-mails into stories that are truthful, humorous, concise, coherent, and honest. He tackled this project with limited time and hit every deadline while still giving me a chance to have final say. We are so lucky to have an accomplished writer and editor in our family, but he would have been my first choice even if we weren't related. He gave us the best voice to explain this story.

Thank you to my sister Lenore, who has handled most of my fan communication for the last several years. It is never easy, especially with so many heartbreaking stories and pleas for help, but she approaches it with the utmost respect, dignity and patience. She is a Make-A-Wish foundation in her own right and deserves a humanitarian award of epic proportions.

Thanks to my mom, who allowed me to follow my passion and do something different even when my future in skateboarding looked bleak. She believed in me when very few others did, and always welcomed my unique brethren with open arms. It's no wonder that all of my friends wanted to stay with me during our formative years; many of them considered her their second mom.

To everyone at Tony Hawk, Inc. (THI), 900 Films, Shred or Die, and the Tony Hawk Foundation: Thank you for your collective genius and hard work. We pave new ground almost daily, and you make it seamless. Best, you all make it so much fun that it almost never feels like work. It's almost impossible to define any one person's role, because we all do a bit of everything. I wouldn't want it any other way. I hope you agree.

Above all, I want to thank my family: Lhotse, Riley, Spencer, Keegan, and Kady. The projects, businesses, and successes detailed in this book would not have been possible without their love, support, patience, and understanding. Sometimes my life seems fantastical and other times too hectic, but they have been there for me even when my time with them is severely impacted. Thank you for allowing me to live my dream. I love you and I hope that my career helps to give you a better life than you ever expected.

—Tony Hawk

September 2010

Family Trust

I was a senior in high school when my 43-year-old mom, Nancy, announced that she was pregnant. My sister was a junior in college and my younger brother Steve was in middle school. My baby brother, Anthony Frank Hawk, was born on May 12, 1968. Thirty days later, I left for college. I lived at home with my new brother exactly one month.

Within a few years, my sister Lenore became a teacher, I went into the music business, and my brother Steve went on to college to become a writer. The Hawk siblings had all left home—everyone except our little brother. Our middle-aged parents were living an unexpected, late-life chapter of their parenthood. Soon they were spending their days carting their youngest child to skateparks and contests. Every day. The kid had talent.

Fast-forward to my own "I'm 45 and pregnant" story. In 1995, I left the music business to get off the road and raise my newborn twins, Hagen and Emily. Four months later, Tony asked me if I would help him at his fledgling skateboard company, Birdhouse Projects. My title would be "Tony Hawk Promotions." That turned out to be an understatement. I had worked with a lot of famous musicians, so I thought it would be fun to do something new, maybe even help foster a different kind of pop star. Skateboarding felt a lot like rock 'n' roll to me, so it seemed like a good fit.

Also, he knew that he could trust me to look out for his interests. And it helped that I really liked the boss.

Within a few years, I left Birdhouse and helped Tony start Hawk Clothing and Tony Hawk, Inc. He was CEO; I headed up operations. We slowly built these companies from the ground up, while Tony's fan base continued to grow and grow and grow. I contacted several of my colleagues from the music world, and together Tony and I put together a trusted team of agents, lawyers, and accountants—along with an invaluable publicist. Most of them are still with us. We also began to build our staff at THI.

I've been working with Tony for 15 years now. Together with our talented team, we have created a fun, ever-expanding business. Tony's personal passions are family, friends, and skating. He's an extremely creative and intelligent guy, and generous to a fault. He comes up with incredible marketing ideas, stunts, events, and a myriad of projects. My primary job is to organize funding and help coordinate the production and marketing surrounding these concepts. And many times, even if I can't help raise the money, we do it anyway.

By 1997, the company had grown to the point where we needed our own building. We'd started Hawk Clothing in my family's garage in San Juan Capistrano, California, but eventually moved to a proper warehouse in nearby San Clemente. As we added more departments, we rented more space. By 2003, we were leasing editing bays for the film production company in one building, running the Boom Boom HuckJam tour from a different space, and coordinating licensing deals from still another office. We also leased a half-acre of land for Tony's ever-weathering, pre-HuckJam vert ramp. Birdhouse skateboards, meanwhile, were being produced and shipped out of a warehouse 25 miles away. Once we launched the HuckJam tour, with its million-dollar ramp, we decided it was time to consolidate and build a facility that could house not only the massive ramp, but also the offices and studios needed for THI's growing staff.

Out of sheer necessity, Tony purchased a large lot in an industrial park near his home in northern San Diego County and built a state-of-the-art facility to house his many enterprises. The THI facility holds offices for all the departments, includes a skatepark, the HuckJam half-pipe (which required a customized roof extension), a studio for his Sirius radio show, two fully outfitted film production studios, a climate-controlled film library, and enough hard drives to store the zillion gigabytes of photos, video footage, graphics, and designs needed to run the business. Today, accounting, scheduling, production, events, brand management, fan club, product development, Birdhouse Skateboards, and the Tony Hawk Foundation staff are all housed under one roof.

Most of our employees have been with us for years. Our staff jokes that the Hawk family is like the mafia: You can get in, but you can't get out. We're all dedicated to the cause. But no one works as hard as Tony.

I never really lived at home with my youngest brother when he was growing up, and yet for the past 15 years we've communicated almost every day. When he was young, not only did he skate, but he also was a hyper overachiever who got straight As. He was a computer nerd before it was popular to have a PC at home. He could solve a Rubik's Cube in about two minutes. Tony is still a versatile guy who never stops. He answers almost every text, AIM, or e-mail that reaches him. Off the ramp, you can often find him tweeting or blogging while simultaneously being followed by a camera.

A successful business venture doesn't just happen to its creator, even if the person is famous. It takes determination, countless hours of hard work, sacrificed family time, and, in the case of a professional skateboarder, inevitable physical sacrifice. Most of all, it takes a love of what you do.

Thanks for the ride.

—Pat Hawk

September 2010

CREDITS

Photo Credits—Insert

These photos were used with permission:

Hershey's MilkShake bottle photo, courtesy of © White Wave Foods Company. (page 3 of color insert)

The Simpsons illustration, courtesy of THE SIMPSONS ™ & © 1990 Twentieth Century Fox Film Corporation. (page 10 of color insert)

Tony Hawk's Halfpipe and Tony Hawk's Big Spin photo, courtesy of Six Flags Entertainment Corp. (page 2 of color insert)

Nixon Advertisement, courtesy of Nixon Inc. (page 6 of color insert)

Cover of *Success* magazine, courtesy of SUCCESS Magazine, November 2008, published by SUCCESS media. All Rights reserved. www.Success.com. (page 10 of color insert)

Hawk Clothing Advertisement, Courtesy of Kohl's Department Stores (page 3 of color insert)

■ ■ ■

Other material used with permission, include the following:

"An Enigmatic Treasure Hunt" blog (pages 101–104), courtesy of Lyndsay Walsh.

"E-mail Reply to Tony Hawk" (pages 86–87), courtesy of Stacy Peralta.

HOW DID I GET HERE?

TOUCAN SAM TEACHES ME A LESSON

The day I knew it was time to take control

DEAR TONY HAWK

WE ARE YOUR BIGGEST FANS! WE EVEN EAT YOUR SERYELL. DON'T RETIRE, YOU THE BEST SKATER
EVER. YOU CAN'T JUST QUITE!

FROM ███ AND ███

★ ▌n 1998, I got invited to New York to help Froot Loops, the sugary cereal that my skate friends and I used to eat by the case, radicalize its image. Actually, *invited* isn't quite the right word: A marketing agency paid me to join a team of fellow "extreme" athletes at a big coming-out party where it would be announced that the cereal's mascot, Toucan Sam, was now himself also extreme. (This was before the word got banished to the Island of Misfit Slang.)

The night before the event, I joined BMX hero Dave Mirra and lunatic Olympic ski racer Johnny Moseley at a media-training session with agency execs. They told us that they wanted us to stay in character during press interviews, meaning we were to talk about Toucan Sam as if he were real, and as if he ripped. "You should see that feathered freak's McTwists," that sort of thing. Unfortunately, they failed to caution against inadvertent shout-outs to competitors.

The whole thing would last only a couple of hours, and they were paying $50,000, a *lot* of money for me at the time. The skateboarding industry was just starting to emerge from the fiscal doldrums of the early 1990s, and I was a young father barely scraping by as a pro skater and co-owner of a struggling skate company. So I figured the money was worth two or three goofy hours.

When we got to Chelsea Piers the next morning, the place was mobbed—with media people and about 100 middle-school kids. The kids, dressed in Froot Loops T-shirts, weren't skaters or even, apparently, fans of the sport; someone had bussed them in, figuring their presence would inject youthful energy to the proceedings.

We did a few interviews, mostly sticking to the script, talking about Toucan Sam as if he were a legitimate action-sports hero. We mused on how he was a true crossover athlete, ripping the streets, snow, and halfpipes. No pads, just fearlessness and feathers.

Dear Tony Hawk,

If I offered you a million dollars, would you endorse my new dildo?

I bet you would.

Chelsea Piers had a big halfpipe at the time, and Dave and I did a demo for the crowd, with Johnny as emcee. One problem: Skateboard and BMX tricks have strange names (stale fish, Madonna, slob air, can-can, tailwhip) and Johnny didn't know any of them. So he improvised, figuring it would be clever to name them after random cereals: "There's Tony with a huge Cheerio!" And "Dave sticks a perfect Grape-Nut." Like that. One problem: Cheerios and Grape-Nuts are made by Froot Loops' competitors. That didn't go over so well with the marketing execs.

I'm not sure what the whole thing did for Toucan Sam's image, but I know for certain it didn't help mine. On the flight back to California, I decided that the Froot Loops episode would be the last time I'd relinquish control to any company that wants to use my name or image to help sell its product. That decision turned out to be a good idea, on many levels.

Stuck Between Coach and First Class

Skateboarding is a strange profession, probably because it was never supposed to *be* a profession. Decades after the sport's birth, mainstream America still dismissed it as a fad, a kid's game, a joke. That condescension pushed serious skaters even deeper underground, where they thrived, happy to be seen as counterculture punks. They knew how hard it was to master, and how satisfying; they didn't need affirmation from above. Hard-core skaters were (still are) artists of the purist sort. They do it because they love it, not because they crave recognition or need money.

All of which has placed me in a treacherous middle space—balanced on a tightrope stretched between opposing forces, both of them skeptical. For many years, few adults took my career seriously. Even now, businessmen on airplanes frown when they see me carry a skateboard into first class. At the same time, there will always be a certain segment of skaters who write me off me as a sellout. On the same airplane, they'd give me shit for not riding with them back in coach. But I don't stress about

Me, riding on my very first skateboard, given to me by my brother Steve.

the haters as much as I used to. Most of them have never met me and have no idea how much I love to skate, or how much time I still spend doing it, or how essential it is to my sense of self.

At its heart, that's what this book is about, or at least what I hope it's about: how to sell celebrity and promote skateboarding without selling out. For me, it starts and ends with my skateboard, and with the many friends the sport has brought into my life. When I'm torn between business deals, I always seem to pick the one that offers the best chance for my friends and me to skate.

I am acutely aware that I became famous, and make good money, not just because I excelled at my particular sport, but also because I've been extraordinarily lucky. Several times in my professional life

I've just happened to be in the right place at the right time. I got into skating when the fad was dead, and turned pro just as it started to benefit from a mid-1980s boom. I ended up on the most famous skate team of the era, Powell Peralta's Bones Brigade, and by the time I was 16, I was making more money than my high school teachers.

When the skateboard industry slipped into a coma in the early 1990s, I still rode my vert ramp almost every day, which enabled me to keep progressing. So when ESPN created the X Games in 1995 and gave skateboarding its first legitimate coast-to-coast TV exposure, there were only a handful of vert skaters still on their game, and I was one of them. The show's producers devoted a disproportionate percentage of airtime to me that first year, and I came away as the "face" of the X Games.

Then, in 1999, the X Games' fifth year, I made a maneuver (the 900: two and a half midair spins) that had eluded me for years. I'd worked long and hard at that trick, but that day also had an element of serendipity: I made it in front of a big TV audience only because skating is one of the few sports in which the people in charge would allow a skater to keep trying a new move, with the cameras rolling, after time had run out.

That same year, Activision released my first video game, *Tony Hawk's Pro Skater*, which would go on to be one of the biggest gaming franchises of the decade. The confluence of those

Indy air at one of
our Secret Skatepark Tour demos
in Missoula, Montana.

three things—the X Games, the 900, the distribution of millions of video games bearing my likeness—elevated my name recognition, especially among young people, to a level I'd never dreamed of. My agent told me around that time that my "Q score" (an authoritative, proprietary poll that measures a celebrity's notoriety and appeal to American consumers) among teens was second only to Michael Jordan's among athletes.

But I really knew the world had gone crazy when I got invited to the 2003 Nickelodeon Kids' Choice Awards, at which the network's viewers named me their favorite male athlete. The other three finalists were Kobe Bryant, Shaquille O'Neal, and Tiger Woods. (A skater beats out Kobe, Shaq, and Tiger? WTF?)

That was when the line from that old Talking Heads' song began repeatedly ringing in my head: "And you may ask yourself, 'Well, how did I get here?'"

There's a lesson in that question, and it's the first one I'd share with those first-class businessmen if any of them were to ever look past my skateboard and ask for advice: Never get cocky about your professional successes, because the good luck that got you there can turn bad fast.

Rule Number One: Don't Make Lists

And to any kids who are hoping to learn how they, too, might someday get stink-eye in first class, here are a few other bits of advice:

1. Once you find your passion, run with it. Ignore what peers or career counselors say.
2. Don't rebel for rebellion's sake. In fact, rebellion shouldn't even factor into it. If the thing you love and do best is viewed as rebellious, then, yes, embrace your inner Che Guevara. But don't let the cool police dictate your dreams. Think of it this way: If your passion is dismissed as mainstream and dorky, that

makes your insurgency all the braver. Do it because you love it, not because you're worried about what others—teachers, friends, that hot emo chick who sits alone by the bike rack at lunch—will think.

3. Whatever you pick, as long as you truly love it, put in the sweat to get really good at it. That means spending a *lot of time* at it. Take pride in being defined as obsessive.

4. Once you've achieved proficiency, take your specialty to a level that fellow specialists can appreciate. Innovate. That's what will set you apart—when you become a pioneer among pioneers.

5. If all that works and you become successful, stay in touch, and stay humble. Don't get complacent, and absolutely don't get stuck in your ways. Appreciate and acknowledge the genius of your competitors, peers, and future successors. Learn to admire rather than resent.

6. Become a mentor. Hang with and encourage the people who will inevitably replace you. The higher you move up the corporate high-rise, the more you have to make a conscious effort to spend time in the street. And don't preach. Instead, find the kids who are doing what you did at that age, and have the humility to let them tell you what's going on.

7. Take it all in, listen to the competing arguments (maximizing profits versus staying true to your art or your roots or whatever), then clear your mind and trust your gut.

8. Don't be afraid to take risks, but make sure you have good lawyers before you do.

9. If you get some extra money in your pocket, give back.

10. Never stop skating.

BUILDING A BETTER BIRDHOUSE

The birth and near-death of our first business

2

From: ████████████
To: <<u>information@tonyhawk.com</u>>
Subject: Question

Did you go to Collage?

officially became a professional skateboarder in 1982. I was 14. The moment itself was no big deal. I was at a pro-am contest in Whittier, California, and my main amateur sponsor at the time, Stacy Peralta (co-owner of Powell Peralta), suggested it might be time for me to turn pro, since I'd reached the top of the amateur ranks. When I filled out the registration form at the skatepark that day, I simply marked the box that said "pro" instead of the one that said "am." That's it.

I'd started skating five years earlier, when my brother Steve gave me one of his old boards. I took to it quickly, and lucked out in two big ways. First, there was a good skatepark (since demolished) just a few miles from my house in San Diego. Second, my parents were the kind that steadfastly supported their kids' passions, no matter how far they veered from the mainstream. My sister Pat loved to sing; my dad managed her rock 'n' roll band and drove her to gigs. Steve loved to surf; my parents would get up at dawn to drive him to the ocean, 10 miles away.

My first board.

From: ███████████████

To: <information@tonyhawk.com>

Subject: GO F*%K YOURSELF

TONY HAWK HAS REALLY HIT A NEW F*%KING LOW. I WAS AT WALLY WORLD TODAY BUYING TOOTHPASTE, AND THERE THEY WERE--A WHOLE SHELF OF JUNK TONY HAWK SKATEBOARDS. COME ON TONY, LIKE YOU DON'T MAKE ENOUGH MONEY--NOW YOU GOTTA SELL JUNK SKATEBOARDS AT WAL-MART? SO MUCH FOR YOUR INTEGRITY. GO F*%K YOURSELF AND YOUR 900.

My dad, Frank Hawk.

They didn't have much money, but they were there for us in every way.

Once I started winning amateur skate contests, my dad, Frank, diverted his enormous energy into helping the sport become more organized. He and my mother, Nancy, founded and ran the California Amateur Skateboard League—which, amazingly, is still in existence, and now, even more amazingly, includes a parent-child division. Dad also created skating's first truly successful professional circuit, the National Skateboard Association. (The NSA eventually morphed into World Cup Skateboarding, which remains the governing body for both the X Games and the Dew Tour.) He also built countless ramps for me over the years. He died of cancer in 1995, one month after watching me win gold during the inaugural X Games. My mom's still going strong, and lives a couple of miles from me in northern San Diego County.

That day in 1982 when I officially turned pro, I harbored no fantasies about making a living as a skateboarder. I think the first-place prize money at that event was $150. Someone else won it. Even when Powell Peralta made me an official member of its team of pros, called the Bones Brigade, and started selling boards bearing my name (and an amateurish hawk graphic), I had zero visions of wealth. One of my first royalty checks, dated April 19, 1983, was for 85 cents. I still have it.

Things started to change after Stacy directed and released the *Bones Brigade Video Show* in 1984. It was the first direct-to-video skate movie ever made, and it helped trigger a boom for the skate industry. Suddenly, I was receiving royalty checks for $3,000 a month. The amount quickly grew. By the time I reached my senior year of high school, I was making around $70,000 a year. My dad believed it was likely to be a short ride, and he encouraged me to invest some of my income. My sister, Pat, who did my taxes (and is now my manager), told me I needed a write-off, so I bought a house in Carlsbad a few months before graduation. I was only 17, which meant that my dad had to co-sign the loan.

As with many pro athletes, my income was not only variable, but also destined to be short-lived. At the time, there were no pro skaters over age 25. Plus, the skateboard industry was notorious for its boom-and-bust cycles. But I was too young to care, and the money just kept getting better. As the 1990s neared, I was earning close to $150,000 a year—a ridiculous amount for a pubescent skate rat just out of high school. I socked some of it away, but I also fed my gadget obsession. The local Sharper Image salesmen got hard-ons when I strolled into their store.

A World of Hurt

Not long after my eighteenth birthday, the skate industry went into a tailspin. The major players like Powell Peralta, Vision, and Santa Cruz crashed hardest, taking hits from all flanks. First, skating simply fell out of fashion—a cultural shift that should have surprised no one since it

From: ████████████
To: <information@tonyhawk.com>
Subject: Thank you

I'm a single mom with two sons who are great fans of yours. I thought we couldn't afford your products. I worked very hard to obtain two Birdhouse boards and two Tony Hawk HuckJam helmets. I thank you from the bottom of my heart for making your boards and accessories widely available and affordable.

had happened twice before, in the 1960s and 1970s. Also, the industry was suddenly swarming with small, agile upstarts who were ruthless (and often hilariously brutal) in their determination to take down the big boys. Because they were nimble, the new brands were also better positioned to survive a downturn. On top of all that, the old-guard companies started losing many of their best team riders. Some got recruited away, while others went off to start their own labels.

Powell took a particularly steep dive, partly because it and the Bones Brigade symbolized the clean, parent-approved side of the sport. The newcomers, most notably World Industries, were true anarchists who captured the skate world's attention with their ballsy, uncensored approach. Powell tried to look cool by making videos mocking mainstream exploitation of skateboarding. World ran ads mocking Powell.

To outsiders, the distinction between the old brands and the upstarts was probably hard to discern, since even the biggest skate companies profited by painting themselves, and skateboarding, as counterculture. Powell's graphics featured skeletons, rats, skulls, and snakes—sometimes skulls *with* snakes. My most popular insignia was a bird skull against an iron cross background, created by Powell's gifted artist, Vernon Courtlandt Johnson. None of it was *Sesame Street* fare.

But companies like H-Street and World pulled out the stops. They openly ripped off logos from corporate America (Looney Tunes and

Burger King, among others). One of World's most infamous skateboard deck graphics had a naked woman in a spread-legged pose—an anatomy lesson. World's founder, Steve Rocco, also got pissed when *TransWorld Skateboarding* magazine wouldn't publish some of his attack ads, so he created his own skate mag. It was called *Big Brother*, and it did a good job of covering the hard-core corners of the sport, amid reviews of porn movies and articles like "How to Kill Yourself." (The *Big Brother* crew would later create the massively successful *Jackass* TV series and movies.)

By 1991, the skate industry was reeling from uncertainty, civil war, and a declining market. My income from Powell had shrunk to $1,500 a month, and I was struggling to make my mortgage payments. It occurred to me that if I wasn't going to make a living wage from royalties, I might as well take the big step of starting my own company. Also, I figured the industry had no place to go but up, right?

I started talking to a fellow Powell rider, Per Welinder, about teaming up to launch a new brand. Per had a business degree, I had the visibility, and we both had access to seed money. We met secretly for months to draw up a business plan. He would run the day-to-day operations, and I would head up promotions and recruit and manage a team. I refinanced my house, which gave me $40,000 to sink into the business. I also sold my Lexus and bought a Honda Civic. We named the company Birdhouse Projects, and we assembled an amazing team of skaters: Jeremy Klein, Willy Santos, Mike Frazier, Ocean Howell, and Steve Berra.

I was still pretty pessimistic about the future of the skate industry and my own career. I was 24—a geezer. It was time to think about putting away my skateboard and focusing on business.

Heelflips on the *Titanic*

The early years of Birdhouse were predictably bleak. The skate industry was overloaded with inventory, and we were barely turning a profit. When I took the team on tour, we slept five and six to a room.

Occasionally, shops that hired us for demos would tell us after we'd skated that they couldn't afford to pay. One guy offered Chinese food instead of cash. Once, I flew to France for a $300 payday, but an unavoidable ticket change on the way home cost me $100 of that.

I wouldn't have minded the financial stress—in fact, part of me embraced the way the skate recession had weeded out the wannabes—except I suddenly had a new incentive not to go broke: in 1992, my wife Cindy became pregnant with our first son. At home, we pared our budget to the bone. I was given a "Taco Bell allowance" of five bucks a day and I was eating Top Ramen almost daily.

I started seriously weighing options for my post-skateboarding career. My first choice was to become a film editor. I'd already edited some video segments for Powell and all of the early Birdhouse videos, and had enjoyed it, so I borrowed $8,000 from my parents (who couldn't really afford it), and cobbled together an editing system. I actually got paid to edit a few videos, but soon realized I didn't have the contacts, equipment, or resolve to make a living at it.

In early 1994, Birdhouse was on life support, and Per and I discussed pulling the plug. Vert skating (on big halfpipes—my specialty) was dying, so I had stopped competing and was putting more time into the business. I still had a ramp at home, and I was actually skating better than ever (learning new tricks, like heelflip varial liens), but no one was watching. I often skated alone.

As a parting shot to my pro skating career, I asked the Birdhouse art department to use an image of the *Titanic* on my last signature-model board. It seemed like a good metaphor: the supposedly unsinkable ship, sinking.

Fortunately, my "retirement" didn't last long. For one thing, I never really took to the 9-to-5 desk-job thing. Per and I quickly realized that it was better for the company if I spent more time in the public eye, doing demos and competing, so the company could profit from my high profile. We licensed my old hawk skull graphic from Powell, and began making more products bearing my name.

We got lucky, because 1995 was the year that ESPN debuted something called the Extreme Games (now the X Games) in Rhode Island. I wasn't sure what to expect when the network invited me to compete, since ESPN was all about big-ticket sports like baseball and basketball, but I figured it was worth the risk. The producers went to great lengths to tell the stories of a few select athletes in hopes of giving viewers an emotional attachment to the competitors. That was crucial to the games' success, because mainstream America at that point knew very little about skating or BMX riding. And since I was the best-known skater at the time, ESPN devoted an inordinate amount of airtime to me.

I was stoked to win the vert contest and place second in the street event, but felt embarrassed when I saw the final show. A lot of world-class skaters—friends of mine—never even made it on the air, while I became the face of skateboarding for millions of viewers. Suddenly, people who'd never touched a skateboard were stopping me in airports and restaurants. Sales of my decks skyrocketed in the following years, and the skate industry itself started to benefit from an upswing.

Bootleg Braggadocio

Per and I also owned a distribution company called Blitz, which we used to incubate a variety of small skate brands, such as Baker, Flip, Hook-Ups, SK8MAFIA, The Firm, and Fury. Most of them were the brainchildren of former pros who came in as co-owners.

Those were interesting times. While we helped those brands broaden their distribution and range of products, the owners loved to stir shit up. That was part of the charm, actually: watching misan-thropic businessmen compete to see who had the biggest balls when it came to breaking the rules of business. It could also be pretty scary, especially when we lampooned mainstream corporations by repur-posing their logos and putting them on skate decks and T-shirts.

Needless to say, we received a lot of terse cease-and-desist letters, but most of those arrived after we'd already ceased and desisted; skateboard graphics rarely last more than one selling season. More often than not, we'd produce and distribute so few of the offending products that the company whose logo got violated would never notice. We did get sued a few times—and usually ended up signing settlement agreements that prohibited me from even talking about those cases. Sorry.

I learned one important lesson through all of this: If you think you or one of your business partners has done something that might get you sued, spend what it takes to hire the best lawyers you can find.

The attorneys didn't always give great advice. A *very big* candy manufacturer once sued us because it didn't like the way one of our companies had appropriated its logo. Our in-house legal rep suggested the candy maker might drop the suit if we agreed to include coupons for the candy in our own packaging. That one we didn't even try.

Legal potshots also came sometimes from the artists themselves. To keep their designs from getting stale, most small skate companies get their artwork from freelancers. We'd pay the artist a one-time fee for the rights to use a piece of art on everything we manufactured or licensed. The contracts were usually just quick one-sheets—a stupid oversight. When my video game started to do well, an artist came after us because his version of my oft-manipulated hawk skull graphic appeared in the game as one of about 300 different boards that players could choose to ride. We had a contract that said we owned the artwork, we had his canceled check, and we had a copy of his invoice marked "paid." But the guy's lawyer saw deep pockets, and the whole thing turned into a headache.

That was another lesson: These days, we always use an ironclad release for artists' works, and we're diligent about making sure contractors are willing to sign it. If they won't sign, we use someone else.

Videos also triggered their share of lawsuits, especially when it came to using unlicensed music. Very few skate companies could afford to pay for the rights to their favorite songs, but a lot of them just used them anyway—again under the assumption that they were so far under the radar, with such a small audience, that no one would notice. Of course, today, in the age of the Internet, skating bootleggers are way more likely to get busted—especially if their video sections are good enough to go viral.

With the growth of niche television networks, we get approached a lot from TV producers hoping to air clips from old skate videos. But a lot of our best stuff contains poached songs. We end up back in the editing bay, sometimes replacing a great but unaffordable soundtrack with cheesy free music that sounds like it got lifted from a porn movie.

Unlicensed music isn't the only problem. After Birdhouse released its groundbreaking video *The End* in 1998, one of the producers thought it would be cool to add a bonus "egg" clip to the DVD version. Remember those? You had to scroll around the menu for an egg that would lead you to some hidden video—in this case it was footage of an appearance by me on a national network game show, one of the most popular game shows in the world, a game show that had not given us permission to use its footage. I didn't find out about it until after the DVD shipped to stores.

We had to recall every copy.

HEY KID, WANT TO BUY A HOODIE?

Risking our homes to make t-shirts and hats

Mr. Tony Hawk,

Obviously you have hit on something with these pre-teen kids here in Florida. The shorts with the key chain skateboard are as hot as the pony on the Lauren polo shirts. I really appreciate you for being successful in your chosen field of endeavor. Capturing these preppy kids at an early age can only lead to continued financial and personal success.

By the late 1990s, my sisters, brother, and I all had children of our own, ranging in age from 2 to 15. Anytime we got together, and we got together a lot, there was a gaggle of young cousins underfoot. Of course, being neck-deep in the surf-skate culture, we liked to dress our kids up to look like mini-rippers. But it wasn't easy. Most of the stuff for the under-12 set was of the goofy OshKosh-Gymboree variety, designed to make them look like dress-up dolls instead of little humans.

A few surf companies, like Quiksilver, Rusty, and Billabong, had obligatory youth lines, but none of the core skate companies did. They worried they'd risk alienating their hypercool teenage customers by catering to munchkins whose favorite thing to do with a skateboard was turn it upside-down and spin the wheels. The coolest kids' clothes we found were made by a little-known start-up company called Modern Amusement, but they were pricey.

In 1997, California got hammered by storms thanks to the ocean-warming phenomenon known as El Niño, which means "the child" in Spanish. My brother Steve was editor of *Surfer* magazine at the time, and El Niño was a big deal in the surf world because it created a nonstop stream of big swells. One day that summer, at a family barbecue, Steve suggested

When we launched Hawk Clothing we featured our target market in the advertising—our own kids. Here I am with my son Riley along with Pat's twins, Emily and Hagen.

that we pool our money and start a company to make surf and skate clothes for kids. Call it El Niño, he said. Everybody agreed it might work, but we had only the vaguest idea about how to get it started.

My sister Pat had been helping my skateboard company, Birdhouse, a little at this point, setting up team demos and coordinating a few marketing opportunities, and she was looking to head up a brand. Unfortunately (or perhaps fortunately, as it turned out) there was already a company named El Niño making kids' clothes. So we decided to call it Hawk Clothing instead, to take advantage of some of the buzz (and products) that were starting to build around my name. We could also see that my fan base was getting younger and younger, with a lot of mail coming in from youngsters who could barely spell.

Going It Alone

Pat and I approached my partner at Birdhouse, Per Welinder, to see if he was interested in getting our distribution company, Blitz Distribution, involved. Like other skate company execs, Per was concerned that Blitz and its related brands would chase away some of its core customer base if the company moved into the 12-and-under market.

We disagreed. We figured older kids wouldn't care what younger kids were wearing, and we also knew from our own experience as parents that children as young as five or six were, for better or worse, already judging brands based on their cool factor. We were determined to create a cutting-edge skate apparel brand for kids. As long as it stayed authentic to the culture, we believed it could succeed.

Without Blitz's help, we had to start from scratch in regard to design, infrastructure, production, distribution, and marketing. I agreed to use my name to help build the Hawk brand, but wanted to eliminate the "Tony" part in the hope of retaining its longevity.

For start-up money, Steve, Pat, and I dipped into our savings accounts, which we quickly burned through creating samples, attending trade shows, and going into production on a small line of T-shirts and hats. Turns out, apparel is a risky, money-sucking industry, with a long and bumpy road from conception to market. And even if you get that far, profit margins are thin.

But I knew from experience that there was a void in the market. I could see it every day as I traveled around the country. Kids as young as five were starting to skate, and taking it seriously.

Short on cash, we put up our houses as collateral to get a small-business loan—no small task. Pat came up with the prospectus and financial plan, Steve wrote the mission statement, and I was the pitchman. The bank bit.

The year Hawk Clothing was born, 1998, Americans spent $5 billion on surf, skateboard, and snowboard gear and apparel. By 2008, that figure had more than doubled to $11 billion. We were at the right place at the right time but had no idea how long it would take to make any money at it.

Pat and our first employee, Jared Prindle, worked out of Pat's house for about a year until the boxes of T-shirts in her garage began to spill into her driveway. Jared, who's still with me, is a renaissance man. His father was the founder of Prindle Catamarans, so Jared had learned to sew sails at a young age. Pat's college degree included a minor in fashion design, so she could design and sew, too.

Our line initially was limited to T-shirts bearing cartoon graphics: robots, airplanes, and such. We'd buy pre-constructed T-shirts, silk-screen graphics on the front, and replace the labels with our own. Shirts and shorts were limited in styles and made locally in Santa Ana. Not exactly couture.

To help with marketing, we hired a publicist, a former colleague of Pat's from the music business named Sarah Hall, who's also still with me. I was already known in the skate world, obviously, but the general public had little idea who I was. As I've mentioned, two big things happened in 1999 that drew a lot of attention. I landed a 900 at the X Games, and Activision released my new video game, *Tony Hawk's Pro Skater*. Almost overnight, I was doing interviews with magazines and newspapers and television shows that had heretofore dismissed skateboarding as a fad.

All that press obviously helped jump-start Hawk Clothing, but it wasn't the only thing. The video game, aiming at authenticity, embedded several skate brands throughout its virtual world, including the Hawk Clothing logo. That added up to millions of impressions.

As my name began to creep into the mainstream, we decided to try to push Hawk Clothing beyond skate shops. Pat flew to New York for a children's apparel trade show, where they sandwiched our little one-person booth between one company that sold Tweety Bird products and another that featured Snoopy. She spent most of that show explaining to bemused buyers who this "Tony Hawk" guy was. But we got some orders.

We also showed at the Surf Expo in Florida that same year. My other sister, Lenore, had invested in the company by then, so she, Pat, and I squeezed into a hotel room in Orlando for three days. At least now we were showing the line to the right crowd. At the Action Sports Retailer show in San Diego the following year, the buyer from Nordstrom decided to test the line. That was our first major account.

Breaking Rules

We didn't always play by the rules. The day before one of our first big trade shows, the samples for our cut-and-sew shirts (meaning they had buttons and collars) still hadn't arrived from our supplier. Pat went to a local surf shop, bought a few Quiksilver shirts, changed the buttons, replaced the labels and tags with our own, and silk-screened a small Hawk logo onto it. She told customers that the samples showed only the style of the shirt, and that the actual product would come in different colors. This was, of course, illegal. Years later, Pat told this story to some folks at Quiksilver, which has its own pirate origins. They laughed.

When we finally got big enough to rent a warehouse, we looked to San Clemente, which was no more than a 30-minute drive for any of us. Also, the surf-skate industry is centered in Southern California, so we had ready access to good vendors and influential retailers. We spent those first few years printing and embroidering T-shirts, fleece, and hats using local manufacturers. It was a ton of work, and for the most part a family affair. Pat ran the business, and her husband, Alan, a professional bass player, ran the day-to-day office operations and even shipped boxes when he wasn't on the road. Steve put together the catalogs and helped hire a sales team. Lenore and her husband, Dick, erected and dressed up the trade show booths. When we needed models, we used our kids.

Before long we hired a designer, Skot Werner-Longo, and a production manager, Carol Ianelli, both of whom taught us much and were crucial to the company's early growth. We eventually began to notice that our "Accounts Receivable" drawer had almost as many files in it as our "Bills Payable" drawer. But we were still a long way from pulling out any kind of profit. The problem was cash flow. Any growing company needs more cash to produce more goods, so profits go right back into the machine. As sales increase, the cycle accelerates. Also, most of our vendors were demanding payment upon delivery, while our customers (often small skate and surf shops), sometimes needed up to 90 days to pay.

It's a common business dilemma, and we considered our options. Should we ask our bank for a larger credit line? Bring in more investors? License the brand to a larger company with adequate cash flow?

We knew we had to do something, because the car was gaining speed and we were still learning how to drive. In addition to Nordstrom, the brand had been picked up by such chains as Pacific Sunwear, Tilly's, and Bob's Stores. We also cut a deal to sell outdated inventory at discounts to Marshalls and T.J.Maxx.

By now, we had five full-time employees, and our little warehouse was bustling. We were designing for future seasons, creating catalogs, web sites, and marketing plans, producing goods on- and offshore, taking orders, packing and shipping boxes, and building a sales team.

Looking for a Suitor

In 1999, Pat consulted with an attorney, Ladd Lonnquist, who specialized in the apparel business. After reviewing our books, Ladd said the brand appeared to be a solid idea with a good start and much potential for long-term success. But it would take us 10 or 15 years to see any kind of real profits, so he suggested we start looking into licensing the brand to a larger, existing apparel company.

It didn't take us long to find some people who were interested, but none of them seemed to really understand our mission, which was to build a mainstream audience outside of skateboarding while staying true to the culture on which the business was built. Because of his years at *Surfer* magazine, Steve knew some top executives at Quiksilver, the big dog of the surf industry, which had grown into a $500 million company using essentially the same mission as we were. Quik was (and still is) a respected brand among serious surfers, while also managing to sell its hoodies and T-shirts and boardshorts to kids in Kansas who've never dipped a toe in the ocean.

In late 1999, Steve and Pat drove to Quik's headquarters in Huntington Beach to meet with Danny Kwock, the company's head of special projects. (We'd all met with Bob McKnight, the company's CEO, a year or two earlier, but that was mostly to get advice on trademark protection and other start-up issues.) As soon as they sat down, Danny made it clear that he was meeting us only out of courtesy and that Quik had no intention of pursuing a merger. He'd already met with McKnight, and they'd agreed that he should say thanks but no thanks. But as Pat and Steve told the story of Hawk Clothing's swift rise, and of the success the brand was having in Middle America, it was like a switch flicked on in Danny's head.

Here's how Danny told the story 10 years later: "The only reason I even met with them was because Steve was a bro and I had to do the polite thing. So I walked into the room thinking, 'How am I going to tell these guys thanks but no thanks without hurting their feelings?' But as they gave their pitch, it brought me back to the early days at Quik, when we also had a little warehouse with the single roll-up door. And I was pleasantly surprised by Hawk Clothing's designs—they had the sizing down, the graphics, the colors. They were honed in to the under-12 market.

"Quik had struggled with that age group. To get into that market, we'd have had to start a new brand, and that's a huge struggle. And here was one already dialed in, attached to a person with deep roots in skateboarding. It stayed true to the sport's core values but also had potential to scale. And I realized this was one of those rare feel-good business opportunities, where you can partner with people you respect and who have the same passion and vision.

"So I went back to Bob and said, 'My intuition tells me we should do this deal. I think this could blow up.' Bob thought I was spun, and the marketing guys were all, 'What are you tripping on?' But, you know, the easy answer is always no. So we did it, and it worked. It ended up being a big feather in my cap personally at Quik."

Within six months, we were signing papers, and Quiksilver became the owner of Hawk Clothing. We initially hoped to license the brand, not sell it. But Quik was only interested in buying the whole company, so we cut a deal that included a purchase price and future royalties. Although the deal has worked out well in the long run, and Quiksilver has been fair, if we had it to do over again, we wouldn't have allowed a larger company to take ownership of the brand, which in this case included the "Tony Hawk" trademark for apparel. And that's one piece of advice I give all the time: Never sell full ownership of your name to anyone for any reason, no matter what the price.

Quik also signed a separate endorsement deal with me, paying me to wear their Quiksilver-branded clothes and appear in their ads. (I'd approached Quik in the 1980s about a sponsorship, but they turned me down; skating wasn't big enough at the time, I guess.) I

From: ██████████
To: <Information@tonyhawk.com>
Subject: thank you

My husband was just laid off from a company where he worked for 12 years. Today I went to Kohl's because my 10-year-old needed new sneakers. I told him I could only spend about $20. He was able to find some Tony Hawk shoes that were on sale and came to only $19.44, after tax. As a parent, I don't want my kids to look like their parents don't have a lot of money. So thank you for making cool clothes at a reasonable price.

was stoked to join Quik's team of athletes: It's a solid company run by people who know and care about the surf, skate, and snowboard cultures. Ten years later, as I write this book, they're still my clothing sponsor.

The transition to Quik was amazingly seamless; we lived in the same world. The company also had an army of talented designers with years of experience creating action sports-inspired apparel that's both fashionable and functional. They kept up with trends, and went to great efforts to keep their brands authentic and edgy. Although their origins were rooted in surfing, they'd been making clothes for skaters and snowboarders for years. It was an easy fit.

Quiksilver distributed Hawk Clothing to specialty retailers and department stores throughout the United States, and also expanded into Europe. As a result, the brand grew steadily over the next five years.

Going to the Masses

In 2005, the Kohl's department store chain cut a deal with Quiksilver to offer a full line of adult- and kid-size Hawk apparel exclusively through its massive chain of stores. This was a huge shift, because it meant we'd be selling the clothes through a single main-stream outlet that was a far cry from neighborhood skate shops. But after attending many meetings with Quik VPs and the Kohl's team, I realized we could extend action-sport fashion to an audience who hadn't had access to it before, at better prices, and without sacrificing quality. Kohl's had lined up similar partnerships with such high-end designers as Vera Wang and Ralph Lauren. We understood the skating subculture, and Kohl's understood price points and how to market to a broader audience.

When Kohl's began to design the first season's line, along with the marketing materials to support it, I grew worried when I saw that they wanted to use my full name, Tony Hawk, instead of just Hawk. They planned to plaster my name across every shirt, every pair of pants, and every hoodie. Suddenly, I was not involved in the approval process when it came to marketing my name, which Kohl's also planned to use in TV spots and newspaper ads. That scared me. A lot.

I trusted Quiksilver to have their eyes on all of the ads and in-store marketing materials, and initially, I was relieved. The first TV spot Kohl's created was actually pretty cool. It showed a guy's hand as he steered a miniature fingerboard across racks and stacks of Hawk clothes. I played a bit part as a stock boy who stops to watch the action. I was in the spot for about two seconds.

But then the first print ads appeared. They featured models holding skateboards, and it was clear to me simply from the way the models gripped the boards that they weren't real skaters. I cringed. It's the kind of nuance that goes unnoticed by the average non-skating consumer, but any skater would immediately spot the difference and call bullshit on it all. Even though they had legal right to do what-ever they wanted with my name at that point, I had to chime in. We needed to emphasize that the marketing materials were just as important as the clothing design when it came to skate culture.

We reached out to Quiksilver and found out they were also con-cerned. Fortunately, the Kohl's marketing people were receptive to our input. A Quik rep and someone from my team began to attend the ad photo shoots, and we provided used Birdhouse skateboards to help control authenticity. My production company, 900 Films, did a photo shoot for print ads they placed in skate mags, and in the end I was happy to see the main Hawk Clothing logo (a stylized bird skull), on a T-shirt worn by a real skater in a serious action shot.

Since then, my relationship with Kohl's has been great, and they've expanded into such categories as hats, belts, underwear, pajamas, socks, and backpacks. Eventually my company, Tony Hawk Inc., penned separate licensing deals with Kohl's for a full line of footwear and wristwatches. In those deals, I didn't sell the brand, just gave them the license to sell stuff with my name on it.

I also appreciate that Kohl's and Quiksilver have supported many of my other outside initiatives, including sponsoring my HuckJam and Birdhouse Tours. And they've been generous sponsors at fundraisers for my charity, the Tony Hawk Foundation, which builds skateparks in low-income communities.

I suppose the big lesson here is that if you're looking to forge an ongoing business partnership with a bigger company, and you have a choice between suitors, go with the one that you trust will continue to respect your expertise, and who will make adjustments based on your suggestions. In that regard, we scored with Quiksilver, and then later with Kohl's.

"IS TONY HAWK A REAL PERSON?"

From motion capture to gaming franchise

4

Dear Tony,
Your videogame is great, but you should try skateboarding. I mean I know you are good in the game, but you should try it in real life. I bet that you would be pretty good.

n early 1997, I was approached by a software programmer about doing a skateboarding video game for PCs. I'd always been a computer and video game geek, and of course I gravitated toward any digitized version of skating. The first, Atari's *720 Degrees* arcade game, came out in 1986, and I was addicted to it. The next year, Electronic Arts brought out *Skate or Die!* for the Commodore 64, one of the original desktop computers, which finally gave me a chance to play a skateboarding game at home.

It took 10 years for another decent skate game to land: Sega's *Top Skater*, a huge device available only in arcades. You stood on a skateboard, held on to rails, and controlled the virtual rider with your feet as he sped downhill. It was mostly a racing game, though—not really a skate game. And you needed to pour a long stream of quarters into it.

The programmer who approached me was in the *very* early stages of creating a software engine for a skateboarding game, and he needed to partner with an established developer. I was pretty sure that with my help we could create something substantial. We took meetings with a few big companies, including Midway and Nintendo, but they were resoundingly discouraging.

An early meeting with Midway was both disheartening and humiliating, as if we were being grilled by a group of professors who doubted our central thesis—that a skateboarding video game might be profitable. For an hour, they questioned every assertion we made. They said skateboarding wasn't popular enough, that skate tricks wouldn't translate to video game controls. Nintendo rejected us with more tact, but they also showed zero interest. After those meetings, the programmer simply gave up and wished me luck.

But the exercise planted a seed. The more I looked into it, the more I became convinced that technology had advanced enough to create a video game that would attract hard-core skaters and maybe even the general public. And while those first few meetings had felt to me like lynchings, apparently word got around that I was interested in working on a skateboarding video game from the ground up. Within a year, I started receiving some encouraging phone calls.

Before long, I was on a plane to New York to meet with Take-Two (future publishers of *Grand Theft Auto*). I liked what I saw, but they had a long way to go, and it seemed to me that their game direction was uncertain.

From Apocalypse to Genesis

In September of 1998, I got a call from a consultant in L.A. who was working with Activision in Santa Monica. He asked if I would meet with them and their development subcontractor, Neversoft, about a game they already had in the works. They were focused on designing the game for PlayStation. Although PlayStation was clearly the most popular platform at that point, I was leery. I owned and played the three main consoles available of the era—Nintendo 64, PlayStation, and Dreamcast—but liked Nintendo's best because of its graphics.

But the meeting went well, and I was immediately impressed. For one thing, there were a lot of serious skaters on the Neversoft design team, and they were insistent that the characters resemble real skaters doing real tricks. Also, they'd done some demographic research and understood that skateboarding had the best marketing potential among the various action sports. Unlike surfing and snowboarding, skaters were geographically widespread, and they tended to be more devoted than the other subcultures.

Although the game was in the early stages, the controls were intuitive and the engine was perfect for skateboarding. (Neversoft had originally designed it for a game called *Apocalypse*, starring Bruce Willis, but that one flopped.) I was confident that with my input this could be the best skateboarding video game ever created. I agreed to put my name on it and start working.

First, though, we had to work out the financial details. Activision offered me a one-time buyout for the permanent use of my name and likeness on the game. It was a substantial amount of money, and my agent at the time encouraged me to take it, even though a royalty deal (in which I'd get a percentage of every game sold) would earn me more money in the long run if the game turned out to be a hit.

Fortunately, my income-to-mortgage ratio had finally reached a manageable stage, so I wasn't desperate for cash. Also, I could feel it in my bones that the game had potential to be a bestseller. I turned down their offer of a one-time buyout and gambled on royalties instead.

That turned out to be the best financial decision I've ever made. Within two years, I'd made 10 times their initial offer.

Birth of a Genre

We spent more than a year in development. Every time Activision released a new "build," I played it all the way through and gave feedback. It was important to me that that we populate the virtual world with real skaters (meaning real-life pros) wearing real skate clothes, skating at real skate spots, and riding real gear adorned with real logos. But beyond style, I also wanted to make sure the tricks themselves were legitimate—that if they showed someone doing a Smith grind, for instance, they'd get the whole thing right: not just how the board hits the rail, but also the skater's style and positioning.

"The coolest thing for us was that Tony was game-savvy," Dave Stohl, who oversaw production of the game for Activision, said in a recent interview. "We were totally surprised. Neversoft did an awesome job—the magic was theirs. But Tony was more involved as a licensor than anyone I've ever seen, before or since."

I picked a group of pro skaters to include as characters, largely based on their skills, personalities, and diversity. I felt like our roster represented skateboarding well. Each one got to pick his or her own outfit and special trick, and I was thankful that they all trusted my instinct even if they hadn't seen the game before agreeing to be included. (In the first couple of releases, each pro got a cut of the royalties, and they made some pretty good money.)

To get the skaters to look as realistic as possible, we tried to use motion-capture filming. We wore funny suits with iridescent balls attached to pivotal body parts. As we skated, an array of stationary cameras would record every move from about two dozen different angles. A computer would compile the various perspectives and churn out a 3-D rendering. Mocap was still in its infancy, so it didn't work out exactly as planned. I bailed on one run and my runaway board slammed into a camera. It took them four hours to recalibrate the system.

In the end, the mocap didn't translate well to what Neversoft had already programmed, and the animators ended up mainly depending on existing skate footage for reference. But they were so good that nobody could tell the difference. By luck, I landed my first 900 just weeks before

The skin-tight "mocap," or motion capture, suit is as unflattering as it is uncomfortable.

the game went to final submission, and they managed to animate it using video footage and squeezed it in at the last minute.

The music was another important aspect. We were already in uncharted territory, so Activision gave us permission to use the music that had been skateboarding's soundtrack in the late 1970s and early 1980s: punk rock. I was stoked to expose a new crowd to the tunes I'd grown up with, and the first two versions of the game featured bands like the Dead Kennedys, Suicidal Tendencies, The Vandals, Bad Religion, and Rage Against the Machine. We didn't have to rely on hits or shell out outlandish licensing fees, because the game was all about skateboarding. We were proud of our counterculture pursuit, and these were its anthems.

Activision released *Tony Hawk's Pro Skater* in 1999. By the time it hit the shelves, I was more excited than nervous. I was confident it would be well received because I'd played it so much and had shown it to friends whose opinions I trusted—people who'd tell me the truth if they thought it sucked. Everyone who tested it liked that they could make the riders do actual tricks, that they could roam freely around the various skate landscapes, and that the central goal was to complete original tricks and improve your own performance. Unlike other sports video games available at that time, it wasn't about beating someone else, or even the machine—although that was an option if you wanted it. You were basically competing with yourself, just like all skaters do every day.

I also had confidence that it would find an audience beyond the action-sports world. The graphics were good, the action was good, the music was good—a complete package.

Looking back, I'm still not sure if I was prescient, or just really, really lucky. More of the latter, probably. Either way, the game was a hit. It won a

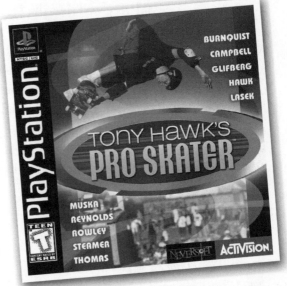

This is the cover for my very first video game, *Tony Hawk's Pro Skater*. *Courtesy of Activision.*

Hi Tony:

My roommate is a very talented film student. Your stupid video game ruined his life. He locked himself in his room for two weeks and would not leave until he beat the game, and as a result he failed out of college. We're wondering if you'd pick up his share of the rent?

bunch of industry awards (Action Game of the Year from *Electronic Gaming Monthly* magazine, PlayStation Game of the Year from CNET's gamecenter.com, among others).

"For Activision, *THPS* was *the* game," Stohl said. "The initial expectations were that we'd sell 500,000 to 700,000 units. But then we released it, and every week the buzz kept growing and growing. You could see it spreading through word of mouth."

It ended up selling more than 7 million copies.

The first release did very well, but the second release, *Tony Hawk's Pro Skater 2*, was an even bigger hit, especially among serious gamers. According to the review-aggregation web site Metacritic.com, *THPS2* was the best-reviewed video game of the decade, with an average rating of 98 out of 100. It was the second-best selling game of 2000, and at one point was No. 1 on the bestseller list while the first game was still in the top five. Activision sold more than 6.5 million copies of the second game in the first three years of its release.

From 1999 to 2007, Activision released at least one game a year:

1999 *Tony Hawk's Pro Skater*
2000 *Tony Hawk's Pro Skater 2*
2001 *Tony Hawk's Pro Skater 3*
2002 *Tony Hawk's Pro Skater 4*
2003 *Tony Hawk's Underground*
2004 *Tony Hawk's Underground 2*
2005 *Tony Hawk's American Wasteland*

Tony,

You might benefit from naming your video games in a way that would offend fewer American parents. "American Wasteland"—my ass. Tony Hawk's whole f'in life is a waste. Leave America. You are not f'in worthy! You little f'n punk.

2006 *Tony Hawk's Project 8* (and *Tony Hawk's Downhill Jam* for Wii)
2007 *Tony Hawk's Proving Ground*

The games spawned a steady stream of competing action-sports titles vying for a share of this new market, and I'm still proud to have helped create a gaming genre that helped to solidify skating's place as a legitimate sport—in the real world as well as the virtual world. And despite an ever-growing list of competitors, the *THPS* series remains the best selling action-sports franchise of all time.

Kicking the Reset Button

After eight years, the Neversoft development team was feeling burned out on the Tony Hawk skateboarding game control scheme. I don't blame them. Also, they were shifting focus to the amazingly successful *Guitar Hero* game.

But I wanted to jumpstart the game, so I brought an idea to Activision that had been rolling around in my head for a few years: make a skateboard-shaped controller that people could stand on to control what they see on screen. The industry was already moving in that direction, with motion-based controllers like Nintendo's Wii and peripheral-based games like *Guitar Hero* and *Garage Band*.

I ran the idea by Dave Stohl, now the company's executive vice president of studios. Dave jumped on it. He put a new Activision development team in charge—Robomodo in Chicago—and we hit

DEAR TONY HAWK,

I LOVE TO PLAY YOUR GAMES. BUT MY MOM WON'T LET ME PLAY IT BECAUSE IT HAS SMOKING AND CUSSING.

the reset button on the franchise. I knew it would be risky, since nothing like it had been tried before, but I figured it was like learning a new skate trick: if you want to progress, you have to be willing to slam.

With the new direction, we had to go back to square one with almost all facets of the game. The first and most important task was designing the controller. We went through many incarnations, and Robomodo now has a hilarious graveyard of prototypes in their office, some of which are downright embarrassing. My favorite was a blank skateboard deck with trackballs on it to slide your foot across. It was almost as hard as real skating and would have definitely thrown people on their asses. We settled on a device that resembles a skate deck (a little shorter and thicker than the real thing) and responds to motion via two accelerometers and four infrared sensors. Only after they settled on a board design did Robomodo get to work on the software, which had to be customized for this strange new controller. We decided to name it *Tony Hawk: RIDE*.

Some hardcore gaming critics were pretty brutal when the game debuted in

The announcement of my latest game, *Tony Hawk: SHRED*, was held in L.A. at Staples Center as part of an Activision mega-proportional debut party.

DEAR TONY,

I HAVE A LOT OF YOUR GAMES, LIKE TONY HAWK'S PRO SKATER 3, TONY HAWK'S PRO SKATER 4, TONY HAWK'S PROVING GROUND, TONY HAWK'S UNDERGROUND, AND TONY HAWK'S UNDERGROUND 2. MY OLDER BROTHER IS THE REAL TONY HAWK FAN. I'M MORE INTERESTED IN INSECTS.

November 2009, writing it off as a failed novelty. Admittedly, there were some software quirks, but user reviews were overwhelmingly positive, especially those from the Wii crowd. We sold more than one million units in the first three months, and we quickly went to work on a sequel that would fix any glitches. The new version, *Tony Hawk: SHRED*, will also venture into the mountains, where players can pretend they're snowboarding.

At the time this book is being written, I'm in the twelfth year of my relationship with Activision. Here's a shocking stat: They've released 79 different versions of my game across the various gaming platforms, including mobile and online adaptations. It's been an intensely satisfying (and ridiculously lucrative) experience. I obviously hope the marriage will continue for a long, long time.

WHAT THE HELL IS A HUCKJAM?

Innovation and improvisation on a million-dollar ramp

From: ████████████████

To: service@clubtonyhawk.com

Subject: wut the hell tony?

i sent u an email like 4 years ago when i wuz in ur fan club wen u were my favorite skateboarder. well thx alot because I went to your huck jam show and asked you a question and you didnt answer me so i gave up skateboarding because i thought u thought i was a poser. If u get back to me on this i would greatly appreciate it.

L ike most pro skaters, I've always been frustrated that skateboarding's mainstream popularity derives primarily from contests, when that's such a small part of what we do. In fact, most pro skaters shun competition entirely and instead build their reps through video parts and skate-mag coverage. That's what makes the sport and the subculture so hard for outsiders to package: At its core, it's about innovation and improvisation. It's about ignoring rules.

As proof, let me make a confession. It isn't exactly a secret, but it seems to be forgotten amid the hype: My most famous competitive feat, when I landed the first-ever 900 during the "best trick" event at the 1999 X Games, shouldn't have counted. I should give ESPN back its medal. Here's why: It took me 12 tries to finally stick a 900 that day, and somewhere around my eighth attempt, time ran out—contest over. I didn't exactly cheat; I just kept climbing back up the ramp after the buzzer sounded, and nobody stopped me.

I wasn't thinking about winning. I only wanted to land a trick that had eluded—and hobbled—me for 10 years, and I knew I was closer than I'd ever been to nailing one. The other guys had stopped skating and were cheering me on, and everybody in the venue knew something was up. So the people running the show (God bless 'em) decided to let me keep going. Despite the crowd and the loudspeakers and the TV cameras, it was in its way a lot like one of those skate sessions that happens every day in schoolyards and skateparks around the world: one kid trying to pull a trick he's never made before, with some friends looking on and giving him high-fives after.

If it had been almost any other sport, security guards would have bum-rushed me to the parking lot. Can you imagine an Olympic high jumper getting the go-ahead to take a few extra tries at a new world record? Or an ice skater being granted a time extension because

From: ████████████████
To: service@clubtonyhawk.com
Subject: please tell Tony & crew thanks...

I took my 6 year old son to your most recent show. Wow, he loved it. His mom and I went through a very hard divorce a couple of years back and this is the first time we have been able to do something "big" with just the two of us, father and son. I just needed to let Tony and crew know that you did an awesome job.

she's close to nailing a quadruple lutz? If not for skating's anarchist soul, I might *still* be trying to land my first 9.

I retired from contests shortly after that event, but I still loved skating in front of big crowds, and I still got to do it sometimes— but mostly as a sideshow to some bigger event like a concert or a football game. I figured there must be a way for talented action-sports athletes to headline events without competing against one another. So I started asking around. What if we built a portable ramp and practiced routines in advance? Mix in some BMX riders, maybe turn up the juice with a Motocross jump. Invite a good band. Call it something catchy, choreograph a whole show, take it on the road.

The more I talked to people about it, the more I liked it. So I suggested it to Pat. She thought it sounded good, so she started making calls.

We had no idea what we were getting into.

Two years later, when we finally launched the Boom Boom HuckJam tour, we'd concocted one of the most complex and expensive arena-based road shows in history. We needed eight tour buses to ferry the 60-person crew, and 14 semis to schlep the gear, which included a massive portable ramp system. At each stop, we had to hire 100 more local laborers to erect and dismantle the set. It was a juggernaut.

But I'm getting ahead of myself.

From: ▓▓▓▓▓▓▓▓▓▓▓
To: <TONY@CLUBTONYHAWK.COM>
Subject: Grandma Hawk fan

In June, we attended a BBHJ show for my daughter's 10th birthday.
My mom, who just turned 58, had the most fun of all! She was up and
screaming and jumping around. Tomorrow we are hosting a Tony Hawk
birthday party for her.

The Million-Dollar Napkin

The idea took root during the 2001 Summer X Games in Philadelphia's First Union Center (now the Wells Fargo Center), which drew a sold-out crowd. I realized that the audience didn't care that much about who won the various events; they'd mainly come to see their favorite skate, BMX, and Motocross heroes perform live. I thought it would be cool to create a tour in which all of my friends could get paid well to travel around the country performing together, like a theater troupe.

By coincidence, a promoter named Steve Moore, from TBA Entertainment, approached me around the same time with the idea of creating just such a show. Steve was enthusiastic and well-meaning, but his company was unwilling to put up any money to get the thing off the ground. That turned out to be a common refrain.

We initially wanted to call the thing "Cirque X." At a lunch meeting I sketched out a rough plan on a napkin for a huge halfpipe encircled by a Motocross track that would allow the Moto guys to jump *over* the halfpipe while we skated. It also had a separate three-story roll-in that led to a launch ramp, where we'd huck ourselves 40 feet across a gap, land on a downslope, then ride into a vertical quarterpipe, where we'd do one last air 10 to 15 feet above the ramp. We eventually added a full loop, like a Hot Wheels track.

That napkin ended up costing me a million bucks.

Pat and I realized pretty early that we were going to need partners and sponsors to finance all the start-up costs. Steve Moore put us in touch with a large concert promotion company called Concerts West to help book the tour. He also started talking to Toyota about coming on as a partner. Neither of those panned out. In the meantime, my agent at the William Morris Agency, Brian Dubin, told me WMA might be interested in becoming a co-owner and partner of the tour. We had

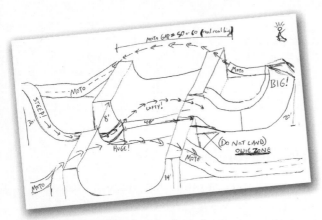

The original napkin sketch of my dream ramp set-up ...

a bunch of meetings with the agency in which we discussed risk, ticket sales, rehearsals, booking procedures, travel logistics, merchandise—all of the minutiae that hadn't occurred to me when I started sketching on that napkin. I quickly came to loathe the WMA bean counter. The guy was really just doing his job, trying to minimize his company's risk, but to me it felt like he took delight in exposing every little cost, and I began to fear he was on a secret mission to

... and the finished product come to life. The ramp system and lighting ended up being bigger than most rock'n'roll tour productions and filled the entire floor of huge arenas.

scuttle the project. Their bottom-line recommendation: find sponsors to help cover the up-front costs, and find promoters willing to put up guarantees for each date, or just forget the thing and walk away.

Unfortunately, none of the promoters we talked to had ever tried to sell tickets to such an event, and they refused to put up their own money in advance. Sponsors were equally skeptical.

But I had faith in the idea, so I started writing checks. One of the first and most important payments came in December 2001, when I wired $10,000 to Paul Heuberger, a gifted skate ramp builder from Switzerland, to consult on making a massive, portable halfpipe. He met with Tait Towers, a set-construction company in Pennsylvania. Tait had been in business for years, building extravagant sets for such touring bands as the Rolling Stones, Kiss, U2, and Britney Spears. I gave them a deposit and they got to work.

Although that construction bill would top $1 million, none of our business "partners" were willing to kick in cash to help cover the cost of the ramp. Couldn't blame them, really. We were entering *terra incognita*. But I felt confident it was worth the risk, so I kept coughing up cash.

The key to the ramp was making it sturdy and portable at the same time. Tait came up with an easy but rock-solid interlocking system that made it possible to erect the entire contraption in four hours and dismantle it in less than three. The thing is now eight years old and has been assembled and disassembled more than 100 times, and it's still, I believe, the best halfpipe in the world.

I'd also been talking all along to a lot of athletes about the possibility of coming out on tour. It helped that I'd promised everyone that for once they'd get paid what they deserved. The initial cast was a dream team:

Skateboarders:

Bob Burnquist
Bucky Lasek
Andy Macdonald
Sergie Ventura

BMX riders:

Mat Hoffman
Dave Mirra
Dennis McCoy
John Parker
Simon Tabron

Motocross riders:

Carey Hart
Drake McElroy
Dustin Miller
Clifford Adoptante
Mike Cinqmars

"Zoom!" Say Gnarly Disaster Boy

As COO of Tony Hawk Inc., Pat took responsibility for doing the show's financial projections. First, she and our accountants had to figure out how much the whole thing would cost, then calculate what it would take to make a profit: how many shows we'd have to do, how many tickets we'd have to sell, how much we'd have to charge for each ticket, how much sponsorship money we'd have to bring in, and how much branded merchandise we'd have to move. Meanwhile, in addition to recruiting athletes, I went out to a bunch of old friends to help produce the show. I gravitated

The logo for our very first Boom Boom HuckJam reflects our humorous take on the Japanese youth culture that influenced the name of the tour.

to people who lived skating, BMX, and Moto. Because we'd be in huge arenas, we planned to videotape the show in real time and project the action onto JumboTrons, so we needed cameramen who knew how to shoot that stuff. I enlisted Morgan Stone, the creative producer at my video production company, 900 Films; Carl Harris, producer and co-creator of the MTV Sports and Music Festival; and Bruno Musso, a producer who'd worked with us on my Gigantic Skatepark Tour. I also roped in a bunch of people who already worked for me at Tony Hawk Inc.: the multitalented Jared Prindle (our first employee ever, and still an indispensable part of the team) and cinematographer extraordinaire Matt Goodman. These weren't just employees or contractors; they were all old friends who I knew would work their asses off, stay cool, and keep it all fun.

Part of the fun came when we tried to think up a name for the tour. "Cirque X" got scrapped because it was too close to "Cirque du Soleil," so I put the word out to some people I know who are good with words, like Sean Mortimer (one of my oldest friends, and co-author of my autobiography) and my brother Steve. The exercise quickly spun out of control, and we all just started trying to make each other laugh. I've always been a fan of Japanese kitsch and that culture's mangling of the English language. Here are some of the early titles that we considered:

• Heavy Air High Boy
• Speed Launch Gnarly Man
• "Zoom!" Say Gnarly Disaster Boy
• Big Air Rocker (No Lame)

At one point the word "HuckJam" popped into my head. So I wrote it down, and then added "Boom Boom" as a prefix, to give it a Japanese flavor. I e-mailed it to the brain trust, and everyone immediately voted for it. In the years since, I've been asked by dozens of reporters where the name came from and what it means. To the first question I say, "No idea." But it actually has meaning: "Boom

Boom" refers to the noise (and heavy bass thumps) that comes with loud music and an energized crowd. "Huck" is a term that skaters and snowboarders have used for years; it means to launch into the air: what you do when you launch off a ramp. "Jam," of course, is an ongoing session of creative improvisation.

Once we had the name figured out, everyone got busy. We were aiming at an April 2001 launch date, and still kind of fumbling in the dark, when good fortune struck in the form of a music industry innovator from Laguna Beach.

In early 2001, Pat got a call from out of the blue from a guy named Terry Hardy, who wanted to know if she was interested in joining him and someone named Jim Guerinot in creating a company to manage action-sports athletes. Jim, it turns out, was a major player in the music world. A former vice president at A&M Records, he now owned a music management company called Rebel Waltz. Among his clients at the time were No Doubt, The Offspring, Social Distortion, Beck, and Chris Cornell. (He later went on to add my favorite band, Nine Inch Nails.) Jim was a trailblazer in the business, helping groups like The Offspring get rich by owning their own publishing and negotiating higher royalties. The big news: Jim and his team were also very good at running tours.

The music business was beginning its tailspin at the time, as people were starting to download music online instead of buying CDs. After a few meetings, Jim, Terry, and Pat decided to form a management agency for alt-sports stars like Kelly Slater and Bam Margera. Almost as an afterthought, Jim mentioned that he'd also be happy to help with the Boom Boom HuckJam show. Before we knew it, his people were on the phone booking the tour, and suddenly we had a partner who knew what he was doing, and who was willing to commit resources to the project. Pat called WMA and TBA and politely told them they were off the tour, so to speak.

At Jim's suggestion, we brought in Mike McGinley (aka Goon), a tour accountant for Sting and No Doubt. We also hired one of Jim's best production managers, Ray Woodbury, who'd been a partner on the Warped Tour. I remember that at every meeting we had with the main team, Goon would tell us we were crazy to spend all this money without knowing if anyone would buy a ticket. But we'd heard that before. So we plowed ahead, naïve to the vagaries of the concert business. In the end, Pat, Jim, and I ended up pouring about $2 million into it to get it off the ground, including $500,000 to produce an hour-long "making of the tour" TV show that would air in advance on ESPN, MTV, and various regional networks to promote ticket sales.

Three weeks before the first show, we set up the ramp in an enormous airplane hangar at the former Norton Air Force Base in San Bernardino, east of Los Angeles, where the other athletes and I went to work choreographing the routines. That was a wild, exciting, stressful time. We were trying stuff no one had ever tried before, with up to five people on the ramp at the same time, sometimes

Freestyle Moto-X rider Dustin Miller wows the crowd on our first arena tour.

riding over and under each other, their trick lists worked out in advance. We made time for a period of improvised riding in the middle of the show—a jam session—but most of it was precisely scripted.

For the finale, we decided to have the Moto guys fly over the outside edges of the ramp while the rest of us sessioned beneath them. That was the scariest part. We actually had to cordon off sections of the deck with caution tape to keep the skaters and BMXers from wandering into a motorcycle's flight path. As soon as we heard engines, we knew to stay away from certain zones or somebody would get hurt.

The Moto guys were troopers. Clifford Adoptante was fresh off a broken femur and had to use a cane to walk to his bike. The jump was blind, with a 14-foot-high ramp between takeoff and landing blocking their view. On his first attempt, Drake McElroy overshot the landing and broke his jaw. That was just 10 days before opening night, and we ended up replacing him with our Moto coordinator, Micky Dymond, because by the time Drake got jacked, it was too late for anyone else to learn the routines.

As we rehearsed, Jim and Pat inked deals with the various performers' agents, and Jim asked Social D and Offspring to play at the first event. We decided to have the premiere at the Mandalay Bay in Las Vegas.

We started selling tickets eight weeks before the first show. Sales were painfully slow. Two weeks out, we'd sold only 25 percent of the available tickets. We were all worried. Jim, who knew the business as well as anyone, was particularly worried. He told us we had to start making plans to "paper the house," meaning we'd give away tickets to fill empty seats so the press wouldn't declare it a flop. Fortunately, Jim and steadfast promoter Bill Silva did a bang-up job getting local radio stations to promote the show, and we had a surge of last-minute walk-up business. That gave us hope.

Anyway, the show went on, and we all had a blast, and the crowd seemed to enjoy it. *USA Today*, MTV, *Access Hollywood*, and ESPN all covered the event, and gave favorable reviews. That night, we popped the champagne, exchanged high-fives, and everybody went home happy. Then Pat, Jim, and I looked at the accountant's reckoning, and freaked. The venue and local labor costs were so enormous, we'd netted next to nothing. At that rate, there was no way we'd recoup all of our start-up costs. It was particularly bittersweet for me. I'd been excited to see so many screaming kids and stoked parents in the stands, but it looked like we were about to lose a whole lot of money.

Our goal had been to launch a summer tour just two months later, but now we were having serious second thoughts. Pat went on a mission to find sponsors. Fortunately, Activision planned to launch the fourth installment of my video game in November of that year. The game's marketing team agreed to be the HuckJam's title sponsor if we'd postpone the tour to coincide with the game's release. Even though kids would be in school by then, we said okay, and began to organize a 24-city tour for the fall, to be sponsored by Activision, Sony PlayStation, and a new pudding-in-tube product called Squeeze-N-Go.

Five months after that first show in Vegas, we gathered up most of the same athletes and crew, studied the films, made some production changes, and went back to the hangar for rehearsals.

After the last rehearsal, when everything was packed, we stepped outside the hangar and took in the sight of the huge convoy of trucks and buses, all ready to roll. I think that may have been the first time the Talking Heads song ran through my head.

In addition to Social D and Offspring, Jim had managed to pull in Face to Face, Good Charlotte, and CKY to play at various stops along the way. Just before the final tour plans were cemented, Jim asked me, "What do you think about Devo?" I thought he was joking. Devo had been one of my favorite bands growing up. They were deeply connected to the underground skate scene of the early 1980s, but I'd never had a chance to see them play because I was so young, and they hadn't toured in years. I thought Jim was crazy, but he said, "I'll call Mark." *Meaning Mark Mothersbaugh, the band's co-founder?* In my mind, that was the equivalent of saying, "Maybe we should get Zep—I'll call Robert and Jimmie." Devo ended up playing two dates with us, Anaheim and my hometown of San Diego. When they played the SD show, it was my dream demo: friends and family in the crowd and one of my favorite bands playing *on the deck*. That night, I pulled my first 900 of the tour.

Trial by Fire—and by the Loop of Death

It didn't take long to realize, though, that our plans for the first HuckJam tour were stupidly ambitious: too many big-name bands (with their crews, gear, and personalized sound checks) and too many goofy sideshows each night. During set changes, for instance, we had mimes sweep the ramps with giant brooms, hot models in skin-tight space suits walking around with signs introducing each show segment, and a weird mid-arena lounge area where the athletes were supposed to relax between sessions while being interviewed by emcees.

On top of all that, our ramp system covered the entire arena floor, which meant that at each venue we had to install lights to illuminate about four times more space than the typical rock band. And that, of course, required more workers and more money. The first few dress rehearsals were incredibly dangerous, with airborne motorcycles just missing crew members running to change sets. We ended up using spotters and buying red-yellow-green stoplights to avoid mishaps.

Also, we were so thankful to have sponsors that we made some embarrassing compromises to keep them happy. We initially agreed to give out free Squeeze-N-Go pudding samples during intermission, and to have our emcee, Rick Thorne, lead the audience in a "SQUEEZE AND GO!" chant. That made everybody cringe, including most of the spectators, so I asked Pat to tell the Squeeze-N-Go people that we needed to kill the chant. Before the second tour started, BMX star Dave Mirra went through all of the rehearsals, collected his rehearsal pay, and then, on the day before we were flying out, announced that he was leaving to host a reality show on MTV. That was about as pissed as I've ever been, because he'd kept it a secret and because his replacement wouldn't have time to memorize our routines, which put all of the performers at risk. In another stroke of luck, we persuaded BMX legend Dennis McCoy (who had been cut earlier to make room for a newer rider) to sub for Mirra. Dennis hopped on a plane in Kansas City, studied the routines on video while flying, learned them in one day, and kicked ass the whole tour. He remains a key HuckJam performer to this day.

As the tours progressed, we experimented with more complicated routines that included BMX and skate simultaneously. Andy, Lincoln, K-Rob, and I even attempted a quadruple stack, in which we tried to ride above and below each other on the same side of the ramp at the same instant. Kevin came down on Andy's back and severely rolled his ankle. I ended up carving too far trying to dodge the other three guys and went off the side of the ramp. That was our lone attempt at a four-way.

But there were emotional high points as well. We sometimes arranged with the Make-A-Wish Foundation to arrange VIP seating for severely sick children. At a pre-show meet-and-greet, I promised one of the terminally ill kids I'd do a 900 for him. It took me a few tries, but I made it. On my way back up to the ramp deck, I pointed at him, and his older brother burst into tears. After the show, I went backstage and found a quiet place to cry myself.

By the end of the second tour, we decided to do away with the big-name bands and create our own house band to play covers of our favorite music. That worked out well, and the whole thing started to hum like a well-tuned engine. It wasn't easy, spending seven weeks on the road each year, but the road has its own allure once you get into the rhythm.

HuckJam Happy Meals?

In 2004, we spent a long time negotiating a contract with Fox Sports to film a one-off HuckJam show in Phoenix for a 60-minute special to air on Fox's new cable channel, Fuel TV, the first-ever 24/7 action-sports channel. We also cut a deal with Fox to film and create an eight-part reality series, *Tony Hawk's HuckJam Diaries.* It was mutually beneficial: Fox wanted original programming for their new network, and we needed sponsorship dollars to keep the tour alive. Also, I was (and still am) a fan of Fuel TV.

That same year, I was offered a hefty two-year endorsement deal with McDonald's and Powerade. McDonald's wanted to create a Happy Meal with small skate-related toys, and we talked them into using the Boom Boom HuckJam brand. I knew I'd take flak from some core skaters, but I wasn't being duplicitous: My kids were fiends for Happy Meals and McNuggets. McDonald's also agreed to sponsor the 2005 summer tour. They were promoting Powerade as one of their "well" drinks, so Powerade came in as a major sponsor as well. We decided to book another tour, and McDonald's sold 22 million Boom Boom HuckJam Happy Meals that year. And the toys were actually some of the coolest they've ever sold.

As the tours progressed, it became increasingly clear that our audiences, primarily families, were there to see the action, not see bands, so we ditched the live musicians and created an original pre-recorded

McDonald's interpreted the many disciplines of the Boom Boom HuckJam tour into what turned out to be a very popular Happy Meal toy set.

soundtrack. Pat's husband, Alan Deremo, an accomplished studio musician, arranged the music and wrote many of the tracks.

The tour kept morphing. In 2006 and 2007, we restricted it to Six Flags amusement parks across the country: eight stops, four shows per stop. The next year we went crazy with a manic 24-city tour that almost killed us all.

Meanwhile, Pat was out pitching the Boom Boom HuckJam to various licensees, which enabled us to extend the brand into markets beyond the core skate world, without placing my name front and center: school supplies, DVDs, bedding, linens, party supplies, room décor, vitamins, flash drives, toys, pool toys, bikes, skateboards, helmets, and safety pads. I'm grateful that those products have kept the show alive and continue to generate income even when we're not actually touring.

But—and I can't say for sure the other athletes agree—I'm jonesing to get back out there. There's nothing like skating in front of an appreciative crowd filled with people of all ages, especially when you can do it without worrying about how you're going to get scored by a bunch of judges.

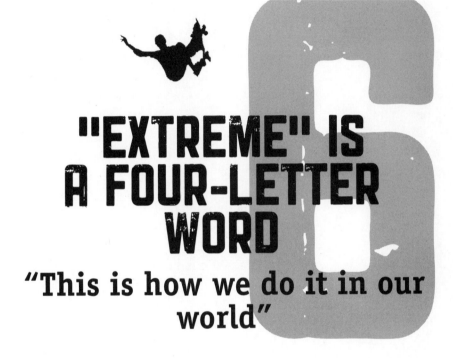

"EXTREME" IS A FOUR-LETTER WORD

"This is how we do it in our world"

Dear Tony Hawk

I am 13 teen years old and I am your biggest fan. I have all your T-shirts, and merchandice. I also have your bio, the Falcon 2 deck, "The End" video, and your trick tips tape. In school, some kids bad mouth you and say you are a sell-out and I look at them in despise.

Sincerely,
█████████

n 2002, we cut a sponsorship deal with a marketing agency for a Hershey's-branded chocolate milk product. My name and image were going to be all over the campaign: TV commercials, print ads, point-of-purchase displays, and packaging. Even though I didn't have any contractual control over the "creative," as it's called, I decided to push for at least a modicum of authenticity, since I'd be skating in the TV spot.

I really wanted the ad agency to get a director for the TV shoot who had experience filming skaters, so I steered them toward Stacy Peralta, my former team manager and co-creator of Powell Peralta Skateboards. Stacy's star was rising in Hollywood at that point, having directed the well-received documentary *Dogtown and Z-Boys*. They said okay, and I was stoked to be working with him again.

But when we got to the set in L.A., we noticed that the extras were dressed in dorky orange and brown outfits. Somebody had decided to color-coordinate the wardrobe with the package design. Fortunately, I'd brought along my recently hired brand manager, Jaimie Muehlhausen, who politely asked the stylist if they could dress everyone in real skate clothes. They agreed, and the shoot went well. I even managed to pull a 900.

As a longtime user of the T-Mobile Sidekick, I was excited when I got to design my own personal signature model.
Courtesy of T-Mobile® USA, Inc.

From: ████████████
To: <information@tonyhawk.com>
Subject: McDonald's

An article in the *New York Times* says you include McDonald's among
your sponsors, and that you take your own children to McDonald's. How
can we fight obesity in America when a role model such as yourself
endorses fast food? I think I deserve a reply.

Not long after the commercial was in the can, the agency sent us
samples of the product's proposed packaging. Like the extras' wardrobe, it was cheesy—an artless Madison Avenue–like incarnation of
"extreme" graphics. Jaimie took their template and specs, sketched out
his own version,
and sent it to the
designers as an
example of a more
credible direction,
saying, "This is
how we do it in
our world." We
hoped his version
might influence
their finished
product, but it
did more than
that: They used
it untouched.

HuckJam bedding.

That story illustrates one of our fundamental business tenets:
Gravitate toward sponsors and licensees that are willing to collabo-
rate on, or even give our team control over, the look and feel of marketing material, no matter how seemingly insignificant. It's allowed

us to weave a thread of graphic continuity through a wide range of products. The same hawk skull that adorns a Birdhouse skateboard also smiles out from a T-Mobile Sidekick or a back-to-school portfolio. It benefits both sides: The retail goods receive a stamp of credibility, and my logo (and thus the brand attached to my name) remains intact and recognizable as it gets adapted to an ever-growing range of products.

When Not to Trust Your Gut

I've learned to trust my gut reaction when it comes to rejecting or considering offers from potential licensees. Every now and then, though, my gut blows it.

For example, a few years back I was asked if I wanted to attach my name to a line of BMX bikes that would be made by Dynacraft, the mass-market bike manufacturer. I initially resisted because I worried that I'd look like an interloper. I imagined what my reaction would have been if a famous BMXer came out with a line of skateboards. But Pat pointed out that we'd already developed a wide range of HuckJam products, like bedding and party supplies, using imagery from skating, BMX, and Motocross. Ultimately, I agreed to put the HuckJam name on the bikes on the condition that the styles and features would be consistent with professional BMX

I had no idea how successful the Tony Hawk Huck-Jam Series bicycles would turn out to be.

bikes. I also insisted that they hire a professional BMXer (Mike "Rooftop" Escamilla) as a consultant.

My confidence in the line grew as the bikes moved through R&D, but my fear returned when I found out that Dynacraft planned to launch the line at the annual InterBike Trade show in Las Vegas by installing a huge booth in the middle of the show's "core" BMX section—and that I had to make an appearance. It was particularly awkward because we were doing a lower price-point line, and our booth was adjacent to Dave Mirra's. I worried that the hardcore BMX industry would accuse us of stepping on their toes. I did an autograph signing, and even though we felt a bit out of place, the reception was surprisingly positive. I was really glad Rooftop was there for moral support.

Bottom line: My fears were misplaced; the HuckJam bike line boomed.

The Last of the Flimsy Pink Backpacks

The licensing boom for Tony Hawk Inc. began around 1997. Before that, it had been fairly easy to maintain authenticity because my only enterprise, Birdhouse, was a skate company run by skaters. Almost everyone in the building had been skating since they were kids; it was what defined them. As a result, they were hypersensitive about producing any kind of graphic or marketing material that hard-core skaters might mock. But as I began to gain mainstream recognition, companies with zero knowledge of our world wanted to capitalize on all things extreme. We quickly realized that they'd embarrass themselves, their product, and me if we didn't gently (and sometimes not so gently) push them in the right direction.

The first mass-market product with my name on it was the *Tony Hawk's Pro Skater* video game series by Activision. I spent a lot of time with Neversoft, the game's developer, making sure the characters, brands, shops, and venues scattered throughout the digitized landscape were the real deal. Luckily, some of the Neversoft guys were skaters, and I like to think that the franchise has accurately represented the skate culture.

Things got much more complicated after the video game's success, as companies of all kinds began courting me with sponsorship and endorsement offers. I was eager to avoid mistakes I'd made early in my career—like the time in the 1980s when I allowed my name and image to be used on a line of flimsy canvas pink "skateboard" backpacks. To gain proactive control over the way my image would be used on disparate products, we eventually created a graphic style guide. We initially contracted with an outside design company that had done similar work for such entities as Warner Brothers and NASCAR. They helped us develop new logos, then assembled all the collateral (artwork, font styles, Pantone colors, photos, and so forth) on discs for licensees. But outsourcing was expensive, so we decided to look for an in-house brand manager.

A couple of years earlier, at my brother Steve's suggestion, we enlisted Jaimie Muehlhausen to create the program for our first Boom Boom HuckJam tour. Steve knew Jaimie from his days at *Surfer*, when Jaimie had been art director at *Surfer*'s sister publications *Snowboarder* and *Skateboarder*. Jaimie's a funny guy of many talents: musician, artist, and writer. (He also created the very funny websites menwholooklikekennyrogers.com and redneckwordsofwisdom.com.)

Many mainstream design teams simply try to reach too far when they venture into the action-sports world: too much graffiti, too much color, too many distressed fonts. Our initial advice is to let the sports speak for themselves when it comes to craziness. We've certainly done our share of punked-out, edgy looks, but always with some overall design constraint.

Jaimie quickly became a linchpin in the THI team, helping one outside company after another incorporate my existing logos and designs into their packaging and marketing material. His approach is gentle and simple: give them art they can actually use, that's as good or better than the stuff they concoct on their own, and then politely say, "This is how we do it in our world."

An example: Six Flags, the amusement park chain, approached Pat in 2006 with the idea of creating roller coasters with my name on it: Tony Hawk's Big Spin. I love roller coasters, and I love taking my kids on roller coasters, and Six Flags makes the best ones, so when we got the call, I didn't hesitate. The idea was to make a giant skateboard-shaped car that spins like a platter while it speeds along the track. They also wanted to dress up the waiting area to give people standing in the queue an action-sports "experience," with video, photos, audio, and artwork.

The Six Flags graphic-design team knew their stuff, but to their credit they also knew what they *didn't* know, and so came to us for help. We spent many hours crafting signage and high-octane video loops, along with a mini-documentary about me. In typical theme-park fashion, they wanted to install larger-than-life cutouts of me spinning somersaults above the ride. They submitted lots of oddly cropped mock-ups for our approval. Jaimie tweaked things and sent back high-res artwork that they used as is. We were lucky that the marketing team was led by Mike Antinoro, a former ESPN guy who'd worked on the X Games for years. Collaborating with experienced and open-minded folks made things far less painless.

We had similar luck with a company called Case Logic, which wanted to put out a line of Tony Hawk CD cases. (This was in 2002, before iPods killed CDs.) Jaimie fashioned monotone versions of some of my Birdhouse graphics, combining that with our style guide. The end result looked great, I thought—and nothing like the stuff Case Logic was doing at the time.

The more success we had in standardizing graphics across different markets, the more confident we became in our ability to control other aspects of our licensing partnerships. When I signed up to do a weekly satellite radio program for Sirius Radio in 2004, they were happy to have us create the show's identity. Jaimie came up with the name *Demolition Radio*. And when we cut deals for cell phones, he coordinated graphics for both the phone and the packaging on my signature Sidekick cell phone with T-Mobile.

A final word on Jaimie: Shortly before we hired him as THI's brand manager, he interviewed for a design job with a big Southern California ad agency. They rejected him on the grounds that he'd spent too much time in the action-sports world and thus wouldn't be able to relate to their mainstream clients. He, of course, felt otherwise. Since working for me, Jaimie has helped design successful campaigns for T-Mobile, McDonald's, Apple, Frito-Lay, Jeep, Powerade, Mattel, and Intel, among many others.

With such a diverse range of partners, we decided in 2006 to begin staging an annual "Tony Hawk Brand Summit" at our headquarters. Representatives from all of my sponsors and licensees spend the day together, allowing us to create a more cohesive strategy across the various markets. It gives my large international partners, like Jeep, a chance to see how the action-sports world works, and my smaller street-level sponsors a chance to see how the big boys play. We open with a video that recaps the prior year, and Pat gives a summary of

Tony Hawk Inc.'s latest projects and partnerships. Then reps from the various companies give an overview of their relationships with THI. We finish off with a lunch and demo on my big indoor half-pipe.

That summit made us realize that no matter how closely we work with each partner, it's up to us to make sure that each of them knows what the others are doing—no matter how seemingly disparate their markets. The idea has paid off in a hundred subtle, immeasurable ways, and in a few big, tangible ways. For instance, not long after we started holding the summits, the folks at Jeep partnered with Sirius Radio to put together a successful ad campaign with me as the link. It included TV ads and a five-page "advertorial" for *Rolling Stone* magazine that rolled in some of my endemic partners like Quiksilver and Nixon watches.

The Wise Old Adolescent

I've been making a living through skateboarding for more than 25 years now, and throughout my career there's been one essential constant: I skate. I've lost teeth, endured concussions, fractured my pelvis, and flayed the skin off my shins so many times that doctors think I'm a burn victim. But I still try to skate every day, even though I'm over 40 now. It's not like a religion or anything—I simply follow the advice that I give other people all the time: *do what you love.* I now make a very good living doing something that I would gladly do for free (and for many years, I did just that). I've been extraordinarily lucky that way.

I've also been lucky that my sport of choice, along with other action sports, continues to grow in popularity. Skaters have gone from a fringe culture to a mainstream success story. Shaun White's been on the cover of *Rolling Stone,* and I've been profiled in *Forbes.* Today, more kids ride skateboards in North America than play Little League Baseball.

And of course Madison Avenue has noticed. In 1986, *Sports Illustrated* reported that the skate industry had combined annual sales of about $300 million. By 2010, that same figure had grown to more than $4 billion. My video game series alone has done more than $1 billion in sales since inception.

I've been fortunate in that most of the large endorsement deals I've signed over the years have been with sponsors who understand how much I like to ride my skateboard—and who see that it's good for everyone's business (and my soul) if I'm out there riding my board instead of attending meetings or doing press tours. It's no coincidence that their sponsorship dollars have helped to underwrite events and products that often require me to get my friends together and skate: the Boom Boom HuckJam shows, the Birdhouse team tours, the *Gigantic Skatepark Tour* and *Secret Skatepark Tour* TV shows, and the annual fundraising events for my charitable foundation, which features a private halfpipe demo in the backyard of a Beverly Hills billionaire.

To me, that's the best possible kind of brand management. Because no matter how much our sponsors trust us to strike the right balance between mainstream and core, battles inevitably arise over the way a logo should be tweaked or a photo should be cropped or a model should be posed. Even when such exchanges are entirely civil, we're bound to have conflicting opinions, bound to struggle in the search for compromise.

But when I'm up on the ramp, those issues don't get access. Somewhere deep in my subconscious there resides a wise old adolescent who understands that such concerns are ultimately meaningless. Or let me put it like this: Up there on the ramp, I don't have to worry that someone in a suit's going to wander over and tell me how to skate. That part they leave up to me.

THE DENIM DEBACLE

Some business ideas that didn't quite fly

Skate companies are typically started by pro skaters who want to leave their own creative stamp on the culture, make some money, and—perhaps most important—maintain their street cred. "Keeping it core" remains the unwritten theme of nearly every skate (and surf and snowboard) start-up business plan. Of course, that often leads to liquidation. Mock their naïveté or praise their principles—either way, most action-sports companies come and go quickly.

But every now and then a young exec will get it right: retain his authenticity, turn a profit, and plant seeds for a new style that spreads vinelike through the culture. Among skaters, Steve Rocco did it with World Industries (although he was more interested in shock than style), Tod Swank did it with Tum Yeto, and Jamie Thomas did it with Zero. In the surf world, Richard Woolcott did it with Volcom, and Conan Hayes did it with RVCA.

I jumped into a venture once with that kind of potential. It was a denim company started by Jade Howe, a surfer and former Quiksilver designer who'd launched his own line of über-fresh pants and shirts—a look that would ultimately be copied by dozens of established denim companies.

But this story is not about success. It's a cautionary tale about a venture that cost me a lot of money and ultimately caused me to sever ties with my original business partner, Per Welinder. But I still look back on it as a worthwhile effort with great potential—and as a valuable lesson.

Per and I had started Birdhouse skateboards back in 1992, then added Blitz Distribution. Through Blitz, we helped to finance and market start-up skate companies and nurtured a few skate teams.

The Birdhouse team and brand was my primary business interest for more than 15 years. Obviously, I know from experience what it's like to live the life of a sponsored pro, living from one royalty check to the next. So I always tried hard to treat our teams with respect, and to make sure the riders got paid what they deserved. For several years, I put my own royalty checks (from the sales of the various products with my name on it) back into the company so we could keep the business afloat and pay the team.

How to Build a Buzz

In 2002, after a run of profitable years, Per pitched the idea of getting into the denim-apparel business. Howe was a great designer, and we had room in our warehouse and office for his inventory and small staff. We decided to invest and become his partners as a way of expanding and diversifying the business.

Both Per and I believed deeply in Jade's talent as a designer; he was way ahead of his time. I used to wear his stuff all the time, especially to high-profile events and during television appearances. Per initially limited distribution to trendsetting boutique retailers with reputations for carrying the hippest city-chic streetwear—places like Fred Segal and Maxfield in Los Angeles. Other buyers nationwide monitor such stores, and Hollywood stylists scour them to outfit their actors.

Howe began to build a buzz right away. (I truly believe Jade should get credit for the last decade's widespread trend to stitch off-center gothic graphics on shirts, as well as the vertical-stripe look that came to dominate clubs around the same time.) His stuff was progressive, and it was expensive. Maybe a little too much of both.

Within a year Howe's sales rocketed to $1 million and continued to climb. But the brand's overhead and manufacturing costs were so high we could never pull a profit. In fact, in the 15 years that we ran Blitz, no other company sucked cash the way Howe did. Blitz was doing more than $20 million in annual sales at the time, and Per had always done a good job of controlling overhead for skateboards and accessories. And even though the skate brands were doing well, Blitz was showing net losses—all because of a single apparel line.

It was becoming apparent that we knew skateboards, but we didn't know apparel. Most of Blitz's experience in that realm had been with T-shirts and hoodies, and that was easy: You buy blank, ready-made shirts from somebody else and simply silk-screen your own graphics on them.

Now, we were suddenly in the high-end clothing business—*terra incognita*. You need designers, pattern makers, garment workers, custom fabrics, buttons, zippers—the list goes on and on. I knew from the early days at Hawk Clothing that this was going to be a difficult business, but I had no idea how difficult. Making skateboards and skate accessories is like baking cookies: a few ingredients and a simple recipe. High-end apparel, in comparison, is a six-course gourmet meal.

Jade started to get discouraged because he wanted a bigger marketing budget and a wider array of products, which meant increasing our line of credit. Per, who ran Blitz, resisted. He and Jade started to butt heads. The co-owners of Blitz's other brands began to complain that too much energy was being placed on this one new business. Something had to give.

Jade said he was interested in merging with a more established clothing company for better cash flow. We agreed that that was a good idea. In late 2005, he began shopping Howe to larger manufacturers, finally cutting a deal in May 2006 with Seattle Pacific, the same company that owns Union Bay. At the same time, our bank was calling in its loan. We talked the bank into a 90-day extension while the deal got finalized.

The Howe–Seattle Pacific deal closed in September 2006. Jade was happy. Seattle Pacific was happy. Per and I, however, were not happy, because Blitz's share of the sell price didn't come close to covering our losses by the time expenses were paid out. Also, with our credit lines now stretched to the breaking point, Blitz's once-solid financial reports were a mess.

Ultimately, the entire debacle was the beginning of the end of my ownership of Blitz Distribution, and the closing of my business relationship with Per. Although it was a difficult time, some good came out of it. I learned a hard but indelible lesson about the importance of sticking to my core business. And I got to wear a lot of cool shit.

Bye-Bye Blitz

If Howe weakened Blitz's immune system, the tanking economy gave it a serious infection.

Like most companies, Blitz suffered serious cash-flow problems once the worldwide economy began to slide into deep recession in 2007. As banks started collapsing, loans became virtually nonexistent. On the other side of the ledger, retailers wanted longer and better terms, sometimes even seeking for the first time to return products they'd already bought. Some large sporting goods chains refused to take delivery of goods that had already been manufactured and were on their way to our warehouse. We were overstocked and underfinanced.

Things got really scary when the banks decided they'd no longer let us use the corporation as collateral for business loans. They wanted Per and me to personally guarantee Blitz's loans, meaning I'd have to put up things like my house as collateral—in a faltering economy. We hadn't taken that kind of risk since the birth of Birdhouse, when we'd been willing to gamble because we'd had no other choice. It felt like we were going backward in our business.

Before the apparel business took us for a ride, Per had been known to run a tight ship. He was quick to lower overhead and lay off employees if times were tight. It was often hard but necessary. But now he was talking about cutbacks I couldn't live with: trimming the Birdhouse marketing budget and maybe even its team. I'd already agreed to defer my own royalties (hoping to get paid at a later date) to keep Birdhouse afloat. Now the whole team was at risk of losing salaries, ads, and travel budgets. That was the last thing I wanted to happen.

By this time I'd already had some success building up my own, separate business, Tony Hawk Inc. (THI), based on a completely different business model from Blitz's. THI has two simple rules:

1. No debt.
2. Whenever possible, let other people pay.

I've had the same financial advisors for many years. My closest advisors are my sister Pat and Sandy Dusablon, who's the company's CFO and my personal CPA. Sandy has taught me well over the years, showing me how to interpret balance sheets and profit-and-loss statements. I know what my assets are, what A/P and A/R mean, and I have final say at every corporate meeting. It's not as much fun as pulling backside smith grinds, but it's important stuff, and pretty interesting once you understand it.

Buying Back Birdhouse

Anyway, as Birdhouse started to teeter because of the Blitz-Howe disaster, Pat, Sandy, and my tax accountant all agreed that it was time for me buy out Per and take over Birdhouse. So in 2008, I wrote a check and became the sole owner of Birdhouse Skateboards, making it part of THI. That allowed us to take control of the design of all Birdhouse products, as well as marketing, packaging, and point-of-purchase materials.

The next step was to find the right partners to manufacture the goods, someone who already knew skateboard products and had deep roots in that world. THI had recently struck a licensing deal with Bravo Sports, who'd had success selling skateboards at all levels of distribution, from core skate shops to sporting goods stores to mass retailers. Bravo had taken World Industries's complete skateboards (meaning fully assembled—with deck, wheels, and trucks) to sporting goods stores and had moved the Kryptonics brand into the mass market. We were already using them to make and distribute low-cost completes and accessories for our Boom Boom HuckJam brand at mass retailers like Wal-Mart and Toys "R" Us. Those sales were going well.

I decided to use some of the royalties from these lower-priced skateboards to help keep Birdhouse and its team alive, and Bravo agreed to distribute Birdhouse at sporting goods stores. I reached out to an old friend, Reggie Barnes at Eastern Skateboard Supply, to distribute Birdhouse to skate shops and specialty retailers.

It took about six months to fully migrate Birdhouse to THI—a smooth transition, thanks in large part to Derek Richardson, the former Blitz sales manager who came over to run Birdhouse for THI. Derek was pivotal, because he knew all the parties involved. None of the skaters on the Birdhouse team was fired. We even added three guys, and in 2009 I joined everyone on a four-week world tour.

Because I had only distant ties to Blitz at this point, I told Per I wanted to relinquish my share of the distribution company. Per would own and run Blitz Distribution; I would own and run Birdhouse Skateboards. Per had always been good at nurturing small brands, and he looked forward to getting back to that business.

So Per and I struck a deal and, after 15 years as partners, we went our separate ways. It's unusual in the business world, but we managed to pull it off with mutual respect, and we remain friends.

FINAL CUT

The key to image control: get your own editing bay

Hi Derek,

Below are the time codes and edits we'll need made to the two DVDs, in addition to a disclaimer (also below) that must run at the beginning of the DVD and cannot be skipped or fast-forwarded through.

THE BEGINNING:
- Remove knife throwing from menu
- 3:15 and on – remove beer and fighting from this intro
- 4:18 – remove beer
- 5:14 – fighting
- 19:16 – bleep out 'fuck' from song
- 19:36 – :49 - bleep out 'goddamn' and 'shit' from song
- 25:20 – remove fight with guards
- 32:21 – blur out Budweiser can
- 37:00 – cut out scene with homeless people
- 51:00 – cut out cop scenes
- 52:00 – cut out pedestrian 'flipping off' scene
- 53:44 – cut out knife throwing scene
- 53:52 – cut 'middle finger' or blur out

ALWAYS SUNNIES
- 2:17 – bleep out 'oh shit'
- 10:23 – bleep out 'oh shit'
- 11:42 – bleep out 'holy shit'
- 12:35 – bleep out 'fuckyeah' and 'shit'
- 24:06 – blur out cigarette smoking
- 29:40 – bleep out 'shit'
- 31:29 – bleep out 'shit'
- 31:49 – bleep out 'shit'
- 33:30 – cut drinking scene

Here is the disclaimer we need ran in the beginning of the DVD, for at least 15 seconds, which cannot be skipped through:

What you are about to see in these scenes are activities performed by trained professionals demonstrating extreme sports.

We do not recommend any of these activities be performed for recreational purposes.

All sports activities should be performed using appropriate safety gear.

The content of this DVD is rated PG : Parental Guidance Suggested.

Given the amount of edits can you please advise when you think we can see another set of DVDs for final review?

y chance, I was in the first action-sports video ever made: *The Bones Brigade Video Show.* It was released by my first big sponsor, Powell Peralta, in 1984. Stacy Peralta, who co-owned the company, was the director. Up to that point, people had made dozens of *films* about the various action sports, mostly surfing and skiing, but you had to go to a theater to see them. The *Bones Brigade* movie, released at the same time that videocassette recorders (VCRs) were spreading across the American landscape, was the first produced exclusively for the home video market.

The movie's premiere was held in my family's living room, after a contest at the Del Mar Skate Ranch near our home. Pretty much every big pro at the time showed up: Lance Mountain, Stevie Caballero, Mike McGill, Christian Hosoi, Chris Miller,

POWELL ⊚ PERALTA

PRESENTS:

THE BONES BRIGADE VIDEO SHOW

Absolutely the classiest hardcore footage yet. Featuring: ramps, pools, parks, streets, ditches, freestyle, downhill, super slow mo, new moves and original blaring soundtrack.

Warning: Allowing parents to view this video may be hazardous to their mental health.

The cover of Powell Peralta's *The Bones Brigade Video Show*, arguably the most influential "action sports" video. *Courtesy of © Powell Peralta 1984.*

Rodney Mullen, and more. None of us really knew what to expect. We just knew that Stacy was excited to show us something.

A few dozen smelly skaters crowded into the cramped living room of my parents' townhouse while my dad set up a TV at one end. People were sitting on the stairs, the floor, each other's laps. Stacy inserted a tape into the clunky VCR and hit "play." From the opening action, when Lance climbs out a chimney with a skateboard and rides off the roof of a house, we were all screaming.

The *Bones Brigade* video was a stroke of marketing genius, and the beginning of a trend that lives on to this day. Stacy and his partner, George Powell, had originally planned to write off the video as a marketing expense, figuring it was a good way to promote their skateboards and team riders. But the video itself became one of the company's best-selling products of that year, and it changed the way skateboarding was marketed to its core audience. I recently sent Stacy an e-mail to get his take on the historical significance of that movie, and this is what he wrote back:

> You're right: *The Bones Brigade Video Show* was the very first action-sports video ever made. My intention was to make skate films based on the surf-film model, but to shoot them on video rather than film, and to show them in living rooms rather than theaters or auditoriums. They were designed for random-access use inside the home.
>
> What was also unique is that I was a former professional skater who co-founded his own skate company, and I made the films myself in-house as opposed to hiring a filmmaker. This was a brand new concept at the time, and within 10 years almost every significant action-sports company had an in-house production facility to produce their own videos featuring their own riders. It became a form of advertising and a necessary component in the PR tool kit.
>
> Also, it was the *BBVS* that really helped launch your rise. Before that first video, *Thrasher* magazine had tried to ignore you, deeming you a circus skater. But we showed you doing moves no one had ever seen before and proved to the world that you were a skater

to be reckoned with. It was our greatest tool in overcoming the magazine's bias, because we could take our case directly to skaters across the globe.

What we were not prepared for was the success of that first video—not necessarily monetary success, but success via "access." Distributors worldwide begged us to make another one as soon as possible. They said it was lifting the tide for everyone in the sport, and estimated that for every kid who bought the video, 30 to 50 ended up viewing it. From that moment forward I began making an hour-long film once a year for a spring premier.

Thanks to Stacy, I got used to having cameras follow me around—they've been a part of my life for about 25 years now—and I developed a genuine interest in film production. I also grew to have an abiding belief in the power of video and the importance of producing footage that appeals to hard-core skaters. I shot most of Birdhouse's first videos (*Feasters*, *Ravers*, and *Untitled*) and did almost all of the editing. In fact, during one of the skate industry's scariest downturns, in the early 1990s, I even considered shifting toward a career as a film editor.

Today, a pro skater's video segments have tremendous influence over his popularity among serious fans—more important than magazine coverage or competitive success. One good video part (just a few minutes of footage, shot over several months) can launch a career.

In the late 1990s, after I'd stopped competing, I began looking into creating my own production company, mainly to help provide content for mainstream networks, which seemed to be developing an insatiable appetite for our footage.

ESPN was especially interested in airing action-sports programming beyond its X Games. Their producers approached me about signing a deal in which I'd commentate at the X Games and also host an episodic series on ESPN2. That's when we came up with idea of creating our own production company and making a show called

Tony Hawk's Gigantic Skatepark Tour. The plan was to take a bunch of the world's best skaters around the country, show up at various skateparks, and film whatever happened. I wanted to show that skating was more about community than contests. Also, some of the funniest people I know are skaters, so we invited a cast of characters who were bound to pull some entertaining crap on the road.

When I went looking for production partners, the first call I made was to my longtime friend Matt Goodman, whom I'd been skating with since high school. Matt was (still is) one of the best snowboarding and skateboarding cinematographers around—a natural athlete who can ride alongside some of the world's best skaters and boarders while looking backward, camera in hand. We teamed up with another old friend, Morgan Stone, who was working for ESPN as a segment director at the X Games. I trusted Matt and Morgan to create shows that were true to the sport. They knew the difference between a crooked grind and a salad grind, how to shoot it from the best angle, and how to edit it all together to satisfy skaters and nonskaters alike.

We named our new company 900 Films. I supplied the seed money and the kick-start production deal with ESPN for the *Gigantic Skatepark Tour* series. Matt and Morgan brought their editing equipment and cameras, and we rented a space next door to the THI offices, in a former bakery. The editing bays smelled like burnt bread.

It quickly became apparent that we needed to upgrade our gear if we wanted to deliver quality shows. So we took out a loan for a very expensive Avid editing system—the technology of choice at that time among most film and television editors.

Blackjack, Brawls, and the Pensacola Nine

We did three seasons of the *Gigantic Skatepark Tour*. It was crazy, both on the road and back at the 900 Films headquarters. Skate tours are always pretty rowdy, but this one was over the top. We had a well-equipped bus and a collection of big, uncontained personalities, like Bam Margera (future MTV star), Sal Masekela (future X Games commentator and E! TV announcer), Jason Ellis (future trash-talking radio host on Sirius), Mike Vallely (future star of the TV show *Drive*), and Rob Wells (aka Robert Earl, whose life back then was an ongoing piece of performance art).

The skating and BMX riding was also sick, with an amazing array of athletes: Shaun White, Mat Hoffman, Danny Way, Bucky Lasek, Bob Burnquist, Andy Macdonald, Eric Koston, Brian Sumner, Andrew Reynolds, Kris Markovich, and Steve Berra.

On the bus, we played a lot of blackjack, and pulled a lot of pranks. We made a rule that every time someone got dealt a legitimate blackjack, they'd get a scratch-off lotto ticket. One night, after Sal had lost $3,500 to our cameraman Trent Kamerman (his real name, I swear), we gave Sal one of those fake $10,000 lotto tickets. He got flat-out punked, and we all had a good laugh. It's on film here: facebook.com/video/video.php?v=1194898751291.

Another time Shaun White secretly poured a weird potion into Sal's cocktail. It was supposed to turn liquid to Jell-O but didn't quite work. Sal took a sip and decided that Kris had spit in his drink, so he spewed it down Kris's back. That triggered a full-on brawl.

One of my favorite memories came during a demo in Pensacola, Florida, where there were a bunch of hecklers in the crowd. After a few failed attempts, I pulled a 720 on the vert ramp—a maneuver I've made hundreds of times—and Sal convinced the crowd that I'd just made a rare 900. They went wild. From then on, anytime I made a 720, we called it a Pensacola Nine.

Meanwhile, back at the 900 Films headquarters, the editors and loggers were working 24-hour shifts to meet ESPN's delivery deadlines. People slept on couches, under desks, in their chairs, and the trashcans overflowed with fast-food remnants and Red Bull cans.

That TV series turned out to be a terrific start-up experience for an action sports production company. Fortunately, the show was something of a success, and everyone learned how to create quality episodes on deadline. It also enabled the people with real talent to rise to the

Dear Tony,

I'm really in a hole. I'm the only skater in my school, and I don't get any appreciation for the two tricks I can do: an ollie and a shove-it. I try my balls off to learn new tricks, but I can't get my ollies high enough. Can you send me some tips? I'm tired of being an outcast with no talents.

top. One of our interns, Matt Haring, was a shy 16-year-old when he started at 900 Films doing odd jobs and logging footage after school. He'd taken video production in high school and was a skater, but had no work experience whatsoever. Ten years later, he's our top editor.

"Can You Teach Me How to Ollie?"

Our second big project at 900 Films was the creation of *Tony Hawk's Trick Tips*. A lot of very young kids were starting to skate, and kids from around the world were sending me mail asking how to do basic tricks. So I recruited a couple of my favorite street skaters, Kris Markovich and Brian Sumner, to help me make a movie to teach the basics. We opened as if talking to someone who'd never stepped on a board, showing how to balance, push, and turn. Then we moved on to more advanced tricks like ollies, kickflips, shove-its, and heelflips.

Turns out the vacuum in that particular market was bigger than we'd realized, and our timing was good. We initially sold straight to skate shops and small sporting goods stores through Blitz Distribution, the parent company of Birdhouse. We eventually cut a deal with the head of entertainment at Best Buy and gave the electronics chain exclusive distribution rights for the first year. That turned out to be a good move.

Trick Tips climbed to Number 1 on the Billboard Sports charts and stayed there for over a year. It remains 900 Films' best-selling product ever—the gift that keeps on giving. We recently edited it into bite-size, two-minute interstitials that we licensed to Fuel TV. We've used different iterations as a gift-with-purchase for other products, and even refilmed the basics to create a separate iPhone app that was Apple's best-selling sports app for several weeks. It may be the most evergreen product of my entire career; there's always a fresh generation of kids who want to learn how to skate.

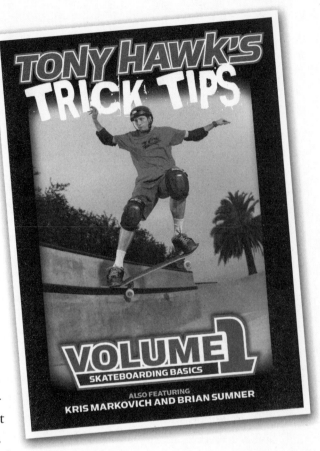

The success of *Trick Tips* taught me two lessons: to stick with what I know, and to pay close attention to

The cover of the hugely successful *Tony Hawk's Trick Tips Volume 1*. The success of this video led to two more videos in the series, and were later turned into television interstitials, an iPhone app, product giveaways, and more.

the letters and e-mails and everyday comments I get from fans. Sure, some of the letters I get are moronic, self-serving, angry, greedy, or all of the above. Every celebrity has to deal with that. But if someone is willing to pay money for a product that has my name on it, and then takes the time to communicate with me about it, I'd be an idiot not to listen. It's invaluable market research, and it's free.

Dear Tony Hawk,

I'm in sixth grade. Seeing you on TV made me want to become a skate-boarder. I can do a few tricks like an ollie, kickflip and shove-it. Me and my friends never say never. Do you have any special tips to give me? Do you get paid for being a pro? If so, what is your salary per year?

My Dad's Home-Movie Hobby Pays Off

We used the profits from those first few productions to buy better equipment and take on other production jobs. In the first five years, we provided content for Activision's *Tony Hawk's Pro Skater* video games, a Bagel Bites commercial, the feature film *xXx* (starring Vin Diesel), a Powerpuff Girls commercial, a Fender Guitar spot, and one of the worst skate movies of all time, *Grind*.

In 2004, productions slowed down and we started pitching ideas around Hollywood, none of which flew. We were passionate about creating a 3-D movie, and also came up with a few ideas for *American Idol*–type shows for action sports that we pitched to MTV, Spike TV, Fox Sports, and ESPN. We self-financed a pilot for a show we wanted to call *Fan Mail*, in which I'd show up to surprise someone who'd written to me. In the pilot, I arrived unannounced at some poor kid's high school, during an assembly that the principal had agreed to set up without telling anyone why. It actually went off pretty well, so even though the show never went anywhere, we repurposed the footage into a segment for the *Secret Skatepark Tour* DVD.

We also got hired to produce a one-off show for OP clothing called "King of Skate," in which various skaters, including me, competed to see who could do the craziest stunt. It aired on iN DEMAND, DirecTV, and TVN. I skated through fire on a grind rail, but I was a wimp compared to Bob Burnquist, who won the

At Del Mar Skate Ranch, my home away from home.

Preschool photo. Apparently I already had a thing for wheels.

The board that started it all. I still have it.

This is one of the first times I ever rode it. It belonged to my older brother Steve, and he eventually gave it to me.

One of the only times I thought three wheels were better than four.

Tony Hawk's Halfpipe a waterpark ride resembling a skateboard halfpipe, at Six Flags America's Hurricane Harbor.

While standing in line for the Big Spin roller coaster, you'll find a history of action sports and an overview of my career.

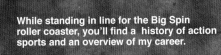

A few of the products I have lent my name and/or endorsement to, all of which I helped design.

An ad for Hawk Clothing that my production company, 900 Films, helped produce to ensure the authenticity of the skating.

HERSHEY'S MilkShake Vanilla Cream

HAWK
HAWKCLOTHING.COM
only at KOHL'S

frontside noseslide

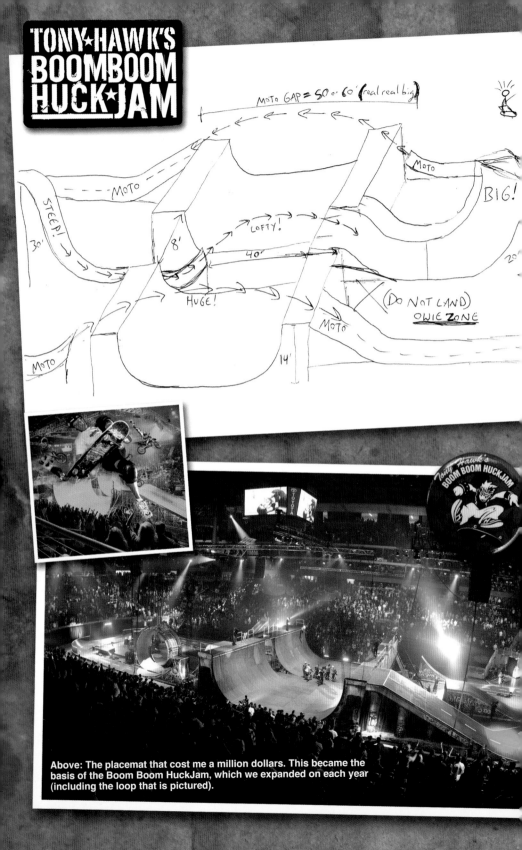

TONY★HAWK'S BOOMBOOM HUCK★JAM

MOTO GAP = 50' or 60' (real real big)

MOTO

BIG!

STEEP!

30'

MOTO

LOFTY!

8'

40'

HUGE!

MOTO

(DO NOT LAND) OWIE ZONE

MOTO

14'

Above: The placemat that cost me a million dollars. This became the basis of the Boom Boom HuckJam, which we expanded on each year (including the loop that is pictured).

The loop is a short gag (and looks easy) considering our shows were nearly two hours long, but it is one of the scariest and most dangerous feats I've ever sought out.

I never realized the magnitude of what we created until I saw it from above.

Jesse Fritsch and me hosting Demolition Radio from our in-house studio.

Magazine ad for Nixon watches.

Billboard for POWERade and McDonald's.

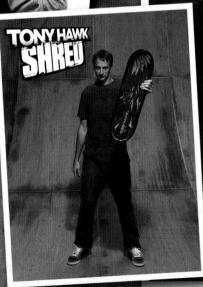

This is a publicity shot for my newest game, Tony Hawk Shred.

Right: Wearing the skin-tight suit with reflective balls while performing difficult tricks is the process of "motion capture." And also extremely embarrassing.

TONY HAWK SHOW

QUIKSILVER

These photos were all from The Tony Hawk Show held in the Grand Palais in Paris, France, in 2009. The show was put together by Quiksilver and featured live music, art, and a full skateboarding performance by me and my friends.

Middle: Me and my longtime doubles partner Andy Macdonald, trusting each other implicitly to not bail or hit each other.

Sometimes we'd make surprise visits to
along the Secret Skatepark Tour. They w
usually too shocked to speak, but always exc

Bam is always a blast to travel with, and
sometimes his personality trumps his skating
skills (which is always great for videos).

Shaun White and I contemplate the drop-in at
Hailey, Idaho skatepark during a stop on SST.

TONY HAWK'S SECRET SKATEPARK TOUR

When we hit the road for a Secret Tour, we don't tell anyone our schedule or route, then show up at skateparks and other locations around the country, surprising fans and hanging with the locals. All it takes is a tweet and a few cell phones and thousands can show up on a moment's notice.

TONY HAWK

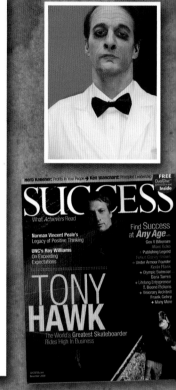

Above left: I was honored to bear the Olympic torch while wearing a few gold medals of my own...even if they are from the X Games, skateboarding's version of the Olympics.

Above right: In "mad scientist" makeup for a HuckJam bike commercial shoot and on the cover of *Success* magazine.

Below right: Animated squaring off with Homer Simpson on the 300th episode of *The Simpsons*.

Below left: Jumping one of the first "MegaRamps" at a promotional event for *The Simpsons*.

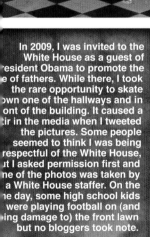

In 2009, I was invited to the White House as a guest of President Obama to promote the role of fathers. While there, I took the rare opportunity to skate down one of the hallways and in front of the building. It caused a stir in the media when I tweeted the pictures. Some people seemed to think I was being disrespectful of the White House, but I asked permission first and one of the photos was taken by a White House staffer. On the same day, some high school kids were playing football on (and doing damage to) the front lawn but no bloggers took note.

In 2006, I wanted to shoot photos and video that would make a stunning visual impact. The shots on this page are from that shoot, located in the Salt Flats of the Mojave Desert.

ht: McTwist over an 18-foot gap in Temecula, CA.

dle: Quiksilver ad shot at our Boom Boom kJam ramp, now located at my office.

TONY HAWK

QUIKSILVER

Get on board with Tony Hawk, Alex Olson, and Christian Hosoi in the new Activision game, Tony Hawk: RIDE, in stores November 17. www.quiksilver.com/tony for more info.

TONY HAWK RIDE

See more at QUIKSILVER.COM/LATINOAMERICA

TONY HAWK FAN CLUB

Greeting fans at a skatepark exhibition.

Tony getting first crack at
a new skatepark opened in
Nederlander, CO.

TONY HAWK®
FOUNDATION

These are some of the kids
who directly benefit from the work
of the Tony Hawk Foundation.

TONY HAWK SHRED PRESENTS *Beverly Hills* *Las Vegas!*

2010 STAND UP FOR SKATEPARKS

BENEFITING THE TONY HAWK FOUNDATION

Each year our foundation raises money through events in Beverly Hills and Las Vegas. I, and other top action sports athletes in the world, perform for the attendees, who usually include many celebrities and their families. In 2009, Rancid (one of my favorite bands) appeared at the Las Vegas event.

To corporate America, with love.

thing (and $25,000) by riding a full loop with the top cut out, while riding switch-stance. In other words, he jumped a gap at the top of a full loop while riding backward. Truly gnarly.

By 2004, 900 Films was in pretty big debt from these speculative productions. To keep it afloat, I assumed the loans, bought out my partners, and took the company in-house. Jared Prindle, THI's first full-time employee, loved to shoot and edit film, and had evolved into a great videographer and director. Matt Haring, the ex–high school intern, had transformed himself into a skilled editor with a wonderful creative gift. We paid for him to go to school to learn the finer points of the Avid system, and he really blossomed. Shortly after graduating from high school, he became 900 Film's full-time editor. Irene Navarro stayed on as line producer, and I became executive producer on almost all projects. My sister Pat began to approach our corporate partners to seek work for 900 Films. Before long, the business was thriving again.

At the same time, I was in the process of building a facility in the city of Vista, in northern San Diego County. The idea was to create a place where I could to set up the HuckJam ramp for practice, house the THI operations, build a sound-proof studio for my new Sirius Radio show, and provide offices for the folks at the Tony Hawk Foundation. Now that I was sole owner of 900 Films, we decided to go all-in and build two editing studios and a film library as well.

We soon set out to digitize and archive all the footage that I'd accumulated through the years, including old Super 8 and low-res video my father had taken of me skating when I was a kid. We've ended up dipping into that archive often. My dad's stuff has been used by ESPN, several awards ceremonies, talk shows, and *60 Minutes*. It's been in a McDonald's TV commercial, and runs on a loop on my roller coaster ride at Six Flags amusement parks. The best part is that a lot of little kids have e-mailed me to say they've been inspired by the old footage of me as a scrawny skater in goofy shorts.

Dust Devils and Big Gaps

Every so often I wake up with an idea for a skateboard trick. When I was a kid, it was usually some kind of combination of maneuvers that had never before been melded, like a kickflip McTwist. As I got older, I'd envision bigger tricks. Some of them were more properly called stunts, like the Hot Wheels–style full loop. Or the time I used a launch ramp to jump between the roofs of two six-story buildings. And if I was going to risk getting maimed, I made sure it got documented. I mean, I like a good thrill as much as the next fool, but I'm not an idiot.

In 2000, I got the idea to build a big contraption in the desert that would enable me to clear a gap between two side-by-side quarterpipes. The key was to make one of the quarterpipes portable, so we could adjust the size of the gap. We got a builder and rented some land and we headed out with a film crew. Adio, my shoe sponsor at the time, and Birdhouse helped cover part of the cost, but I went out of pocket on most of it. My idea, my money. The ramp took a few days to build, and we were able to widen the gap by removing pieces of the ramp. The first day it was 12 feet wide, with a piece of coping spanning the void so I could grind across it. The next day it expanded to 18 feet and I pulled some scary tricks (like a 540) before we removed the last section to create a 24-foot gap. I attempted it a few times, made it once, and called it a day. This footage has been used over and over, and I feel lucky that I could afford to build the thing, pull off the stunt, get it all on film—and not get hurt. You can see it here: youtube.com/watch?v=C2VG8ZtC8KU.

I've wanted to film a 3-D movie for a long time, and over the years we pitched the concept to several studios. In 2006, I came up with the idea of going back to the desert, this time with the main part of the HuckJam ramp, including the long jump and a pair of massive quarterpipes, also set side by side with a scary gap between them. We found a studio that wanted to partner up with us, so we moved ahead, building a monolithic setup in the middle of nowhere. We had cameras on cranes, and made plans to rent a helicopter to shoot from above. Shaun White and I would be the skaters. Just as we got the set rigged, our deal with the studio fell apart. But by that time it was too late, so we tossed out the 3-D idea and used high-def cameras instead.

It turned out to be one of my favorite shoots ever, complete with dust devils and some nice doubles routines with Shaun. We used it in the Birdhouse video *The Beginning.* To see a clip from that day, go here: shredordie.com/video/tony-hawk-new-birdhouse-video.

We set up our entire ramp system in the middle of the Mojave Desert, and the resulting photos and video were spectacular.

Give It Away, Give It Away, Give It Away Now

Things have changed dramatically in recent years for 900 Films. Sales of DVDs and videos have begun to evaporate. Kids who want to see action-sports footage could pretty much get their fill on the

Internet for free. When we distribute DVDs these days, it's usually given away as an add-on with a retail purchase, like the time we arranged with Target stores to include a free *Secret Skatepark Tour* DVD with my video game.

As video moved online, the 900 Films crew began spending most of its time producing short pieces for various Internet sites. It helps to have a small and nimble crew that can get good footage with none of the overhead attached to most high-profile productions. My guys have slipped unseen into the restaurant at the legendary Chateau Marmont hotel in West Hollywood to interview Christian Slater over lunch. They've made a string of online commercials for Activision (makers of my video game) in a matter of days. When we catch wind that a skater has pulled something amazing, Jared will rush out and get the scoop.

As a result, we've been able to create a nonstop stream of fresh footage for various websites, with several clips closing in on one million views. A substantial chunk of that traffic has been driven to the website by my tweets. If you don't know what that means, go to the next chapter. In fact, even if you do know what that means, you should probably go to the next chapter.

HASHTAG IS NOT A DEATH-METAL BAND

Reaching out through tweets, apps, and satrad

Some tweets from 2010

Free versions of our iTunes apps have "dropped." Trick Tips:http://j.mp/cCZGqd Faceplant: http://j.mp/aQe4f3 Hawkize:http://j.mp/d5imUl
9:10 AM Feb 25th via Twitter for iPhone

We will be live on Demolition Radio in one hour (4pm PST, 7pm EST) - on Faction: Sirius 28 / XM 52. Tune in now to get a good seat.
3:08 PM Jan 5th via web

We are live right now. And you aren't tuned in...? WTF! Call us and tell us why - 1-877-HEY-HAWK
4:13 PM Jan 5th via txt

Sounds like a bunch of Tweeps got @thride under their trees this morning. Thanks for all the props and well wishes (and support). Enjoy!
11:26 AM Dec 25th, 2009 via Twitter for iPhone

[From Chad Ochocinco, the professional football player]
Man Xmas is hard people, ,, my son wants. Mongoose bike, are any of those XGames guys on twitter, where can I get a good bike from
8:59 AM Dec 15th, 2009 via twidroid

@ogochocinco DM me your address and I'll send you one of my Huckjam series for him.
9:45 AM Dec 15th, 2009 via txt

To those complaining only VIP's get free gear: I get it. Tell me why you need a holiday gift in one Tweet (don't lie). Top 5 get skateboards
11:07 AM Dec 15th, 2009 via txt

I couldn't only pick 5 since it sounded like a rough year for too many. I chose more that will receive other gifts too. Will contact soon via DM.
8:11 AM Dec 16th, 2009 via Twitter for iPhone

I love Apple (the computer company, not the fruit). I got my first PowerBook when I could finally afford one, at age 24, and I've been first in line to buy pretty much every major product Apple has released since: Macintosh, iMac, PowerBook, G3, G4, iPod, iPhone, iPad—and whatever's next. I think of myself as an early adopter; friends say I have a fetish. (By the way, this is not a paid plug for Apple. The company has never given me anything for free, and, believe me, I'd take it if they offered.)

Anyway, my house is full of Apple and other electronic gadgets, and I spend many hours creating things with them and sharing the results through the Internet. I've been shooting, editing, compressing, and uploading video clips since the earliest days of the Internet. I've kept an online blog and road journal since 2000. I got my first camera cell phone in 2001 and I've been e-mailing photos and video clips to family and friends ever since.

One advantage to all of this technological innovation is that it enables people like me to communicate directly with fans. We no longer have to depend on paid advertising (or the press) to get the word out about appearances or events or products, or just to let people know what we're up to. Perhaps my favorite tool right now is Twitter—the microblogging service that lets users upload brief text messages.

I found Twitter because some of my friends and celebrity acquaintances, like Lance Armstrong, were sending out funny and engaging tweets, and I quickly realized I could use it to talk to my own friends and fans. The best part is that anyone with a mobile phone can get your tweets as soon as you send them. Before long, I had several thousand followers myself, largely thanks to a "follow referral" by Lance.

One day in early 2009, I was driving home with an extra skate-board in my car, and decided to try a Twitter experiment. I stashed the board in some bushes beside the road and tweeted that I'd just hidden a skateboard, pinpointing its location. The feedback was almost scary in its immediacy and breadth. Apparently, people were re-tweeting my message to others in the area and anyone they thought might be nearby. Within 20 minutes, I got a response from a girl (including a picture), who wrote, "Thanks so much, I found it!"

Word spreads fast on the Internet—especially if there's free stuff involved. That improvised one-off giveaway created a little online buzz, and my number of Twitter followers spiked to more than 250,000. So I made plans to try the same thing on a larger scale. That same year, with the help of friends in places like Seattle, Dallas, Detroit, and New York City, we staged a nationwide Easter–swag hunt. We shipped boards to my contacts in cities across the country, and they let me know exactly where (and when) they'd hidden a board in some public place—usually near a landmark. Then I'd forward that information to the masses through Twitter. The whole experiment was called the Tony Hawk Twitter Hunt, and we used the hashtag "#THTH" to mark each tweet related to it. That way, if someone wanted to search for any discussions or updates about the hunt, they simply had to do a Twitter search for #THTH to get the latest info.

I spent that Easter Sunday juggling texts, e-mails, phone calls, and tweets. The most stressful part was making sure I spread the word as soon as someone found a board, so other seekers wouldn't waste time wandering around looking for a treasure that had already been found. It was a chore but also thrilling. I asked the winners to send pictures of themselves with their prizes. Most of them did, and they looked happy.

Two unanticipated things came out of that Easter hunt: First, it got mentioned by some mainstream news outlets and on hundreds of websites. "Well done Tony Hawk for unlocking the Easter Egg potential of Twitter," one blogger from England wrote. "No matter how many followers someone has, they feel like they're getting the inside skinny—information that is not widely available. Almost like being told a secret."

Second, it sent my Twitter fan base through the roof. Within six months, I passed the million-follower mark. Eleven months after that, I was up over two million. Of course, the marketing potential of such a number is staggering—although I try not to abuse it. Mainly I look to entertain and engage by tweeting funny quotes I've overheard or links to photos and video clips I think people will like. I see and hear a lot of weird and hilarious stuff in my worldwide travels. I also have a crew of witty friends who send me links to some of the Internet's best offerings, like twitter.com/shitmydadsays and peopleofwalmart.com.

I took the Twitter hunt worldwide in the fall of 2009, only this time, thanks to my sponsors, we sent out boxes of swag: skateboards, smart phones, video cameras, bicycles, backpacks, watches—enough to fill a UPS truck. We also scheduled the hunt to take place over several days, beginning in Europe and Australia. From there, we focused on the United States, starting on the East and West coasts, then moving in a big geographic spiral that ended in Columbus, Ohio, where I planned to put on a surprise demo with the Birdhouse team.

An Enigmatic Treasure Hunt

Here's a blog posted by a person who found one of the Easter packages we stashed in England in April 2010, from mediakinetic.co.uk/THTH.html:

What happens when you hit that in-between age when you're technically too old to join an Easter egg hunt and don't have children yet to use as a guise for running around like a loon chasing hidden chocolate treats?

You follow Tony Hawk, of course! For those who aren't in the know—he's only the most famous skateboarder in the world who does an Easter treasure hunt each year!

(continued)

I'm a bit of a tweeting novice, and my fiance Alex rolls his eyes every time I ask, "What's a 'Follow Friday?'" or, "How do I do that hashtag thing?" I needed some cool people to follow and after we heard about the Tony Hawk Twitter Hunt (THTH) phenomenon last year, we decided Mr. Hawk would be a cool person to follow.

So here's our messy THTH story ...

Easter Sunday we woke up with the blissful "lie-in" feeling. We're big iPhone fans, so most mornings start with checking the Facebook, Twitter, e-mails, and breaking news. We'd forgotten about the THTH the night before, but then we got a tweet about a UK clue: "A yellow envelope under an Enigma, near a Listening Post contains directions to the prize." Hmmm ...

We figured that Mr. Hawk would want to hide the prize somewhere accessible and free in London, so that's where our thought process began. As a bit of a film buff, the "enigma" clue conjured up images of the movie by the same name—of Kate Winslet and Bletchley Park and the WW2 code-breaking machines, called Enigmas. But Bletchley Park is in Milton Keynes, not London, so we ruled that out. The tricky bit was "the listening post."

Still curled up in the comfort of our duvet, we googled "listening post" to find an exhibit by that name (a "modern portrait of online communication") at the Science Museum. It then dawned on me that this was a likely place to also find an Enigma machine.

So that was that. Well done. We had solved the clue and we could now go back to sleep, read the papers, have a cooked breakfast, and generally chill out and meet our friends for our Easter walk with the dogs. Ten minutes passed, and then the discussion began:

"What if we're actually right?"

"But it'll take us two hours to get into London."

"No. Let's just stay in bed."

"Oh my God! We're not resigning ourselves to old age just yet. How often do you get to do an adult treasure hunt?"

We literally tossed a coin: Heads we go, tails we stay.

Heads! We were up, running around the bedroom scrabbling for clothes. No showers, no breakfast, just get on the road. Archie, the poor dog, must have thought the world was about to end, the way we ran around, threw his breakfast at him, and left the house in a whirlwind, promising a long walk later.

Alex was driver and I was tweeter/iPhone direction girl in this double act. SatNav said 58 minutes to get into London (and probably another 30 to find a parking space). As soon as we had the Science Museum in sight, the gods looked down on us, as a parking space appeared a couple of streets away. The calm stroll turned into a semi-run—or speedwalk, because adults don't run in treasure hunts. Yeah, right. In through the main doors. Alex was looking around like a big kid, saying, "I can't believe I've never been here before." I could see he was losing focus as he picked up a guide to the museum.

"Come on!"

With a sense of urgency, as if I had lost my child, I grabbed the nearest Science Museum person: "Quickest way to the Listening Post?"

We had our directions and after an agonizing wait for the lift (we would have taken the stairs, but couldn't find them), we finally made it to the correct floor. Enigma—where is it? While every other sane person was gently strolling through the exhibit, here were two random adults looking under all the exhibits like they had escaped the asylum for the day. This really felt like we're part of *The Da Vinci Code* now. So exciting. We found the Enigma. I looked underneath the cabinet. Nothing.

Alex now got onto his belly and crawled underneath. If people didn't think we were nuts before, they did now. He appeared with a yellow envelope.... OH MY GOD! We were right—we'd found the clue! We opened the envelope, which included an Easter card,

(continued)

a map to the next location, and instructions of what to say. This was seriously cool stuff. Our next instructions were to get across town to Brick Lane, East London.

All the way back to the car we were tweeting our progress, while googling the next location. Thank God for the iPhone!

If you haven't been to Brick Lane, it's like a medley of cultures, famous for curry houses, pearly kings and queens, and cool little retro clothes shops. On Easter Sunday, it's packed, of course.

We parked what seemed like a mile away, but thanks to the cool maps app we were able to track our way to the next location. We were looking for Oh Baby, a small baby-wear store. When I say small, I mean the size of our kitchen small. So small we nearly missed it . . . twice.

The poor bloke behind the counter must have thought we were a bit nuts as we headed for the counter, faces beaming, as we uttered the code words: "The Suggmeister sent us." I was just hoping he wouldn't call the police.

Bingo, the box appeared. We had done it! We were the UK London THTH winners!

We cracked open the box and checked out the cool prizes: a signed Tony Hawk board, Quiksilver cap and T-shirt, Tech Decks, a belt, a Birdhouse rucksack, sweet Nixon headphones, some Kicker headphones, and Cadbury Creme Eggs. After celebrating with the candy, we headed back to tweet our story to our very patient friends.

This had been the most fun we had been privileged to be part of in a long time—a real adventure. Yes, the prizes are cool, but the whole experience made it for us: the thrill of the clue, chase to the location, all of it.

So what do thirtysomethings do at Easter? I don't know about you, but I know which Easter Bunny we'll be following next year.

For the demo, I wanted to do another Twitter test, so after Steven Perelman, my event coordinator, scouted a good skatepark and got approval from city officials, we asked them to keep it quiet until we got there. We trucked out my big vert ramp. I waited until I got to town to send out a tweet announcing that my team and I were going to put on a performance, but I had sent out location clues the week leading up to it. About 5,000 people showed up. When the Birdhouse team and I left Columbus to tour the East Coast, we did very little advance publicity. The day before each demo, I'd tweet the locale and invariably we'd have a big crowd.

That proved to me that tweets could draw a crowd. I also knew from our Secret Skatepark Tours in 2006 and 2007 that you didn't need a lot of advance notice to get kids to a skatepark to see pros perform. Back then, before Twitter got big, when our crew of famous skaters would show up at a park, the handful of locals on hand would get on their cell phones to call or text friends. The impromptu communication chain would grow exponentially, and within an hour there'd be hundreds of people pouring in.

My most memorable tweets came in June 2009, when I got invited to the White House to attend a Father's Day ceremony with other pro athletes known for working on behalf of children. I got to meet President Obama, and moments later tweeted a photo of myself doing a manual on my skateboard down a White House hallway. That generated some press—not all of it complimentary. Some right-wing bloggers opined that I'd desecrated a sacred national monument. There were high school kids throwing a football around and tearing up the White House lawn, so football was okay but skateboarding wasn't? Moments before I hopped on my board, I saw workers wheeling heavy metal carts down the very same hallway, so I knew my skateboard wasn't going to do any damage. The bloggers also apparently forgot, or conveniently ignored, the fact that President George W. Bush used to go bowling in the same building.

www.talktofans.com

In 1998, before the word *blog* was born, I started posting an online diary/journal on my website tonyhawk.com. The journal eventually got compiled into the book *Between Boardslides and Burnout*, but once I started tweeting, the blog went the way of rotary-dial telephones. The website is now mainly a place to aggregate and connect my various ventures, sponsors, and projects, each of which has its own site: Birdhouse skateboards, Hawk Clothing, the Boom Boom HuckJam tour, and the Tony Hawk Foundation. My main webmaster for several years was one of my best friends, Ray Underhill. Ray had been a great vert skater back in the day,

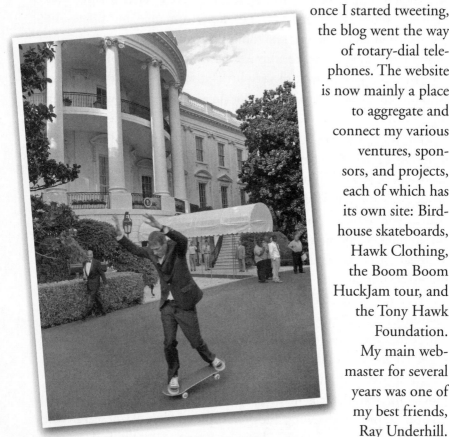

After meeting President Obama, I celebrated with a nose manual on the front driveway of the White House.

and a fellow member of the Bones Brigade. Although he had moved back east to start a family, we had a great relationship. He designed the original tonyhawk.com and tonyhawkfoundation.org websites, and I trusted him to always represent the heart of skateboarding in anything he created and updated for us. He was smart, witty, and intuitive. Tragically, he passed away in 2008 from brain cancer. I miss him dearly.

In 2007, we met with the venture capitalists who financed the successful comedy website funnyordie.com, which was co-owned by such Hollywood heavyweights as CAA, Will Ferrell, Judd Apatow, and Adam McKay. It's the site that blew up after producing and posting the hilarious short video titled *The Landlord* starring Ferrell and Adam's toddler daughter as Ferrell's ruthless, alcoholic rent collector.

In fact, funnyordie.com was so successful that the financiers decided to create a network of related "Or Die" video websites. One was to be aimed at blue-collar comedy fans, another at foodies, and still another at video game geeks. Most of the footage on the sites was to be user-generated, as with YouTube, except in each case the owners also partnered with celebrities who would shoot and cut professional grade video clips exclusively for the site.

By coincidence, we'd been shopping around the idea of launching an action-sports website, and even were at the point of possibly financing it ourselves, when the people behind funnyordie.com came calling. We decided to team up with them and create a site called shredordie.com. They'd build the site (using the same content-management system as funnyordie.com) and sell ads. We'd provide content from our existing library of skate videos, as well as shoot and deliver fresh clips. They also wanted us to ferret out and license footage from the best filmmakers in the other major action sports: surfing, snowboarding, BMX, and motocross. I liked the idea, so we partnered up.

It was a big undertaking. We installed editing studios in my building and hired a team of eight producers and editors. The site went live in 2008 after we seeded it with a boatload of footage from our archives. Users quickly started adding their own videos, and by spring 2010 it had nearly 10,000 clips and 20,000 members and was getting a quarter of a million hits a month. A couple of the videos have had more than 500,000 views. Those numbers are small by Internet standards, and in 2009, the original investors started talking about pulling the plug. I stepped in and took over majority ownership and now carry most of the financial risk.

Even though the site has yet to turn a profit, I've stuck with shredordie.com because the audience is plugged in and influential, and the site itself is a fun, creative outlet for my gang. We've created a channel called "Dissent TV," in which I joke around with celebrities I run into at various events, like Jack Black, Keanu Reeves, Lance Armstrong, Michael Phelps, Ed Helms, John Krasinski, Christian Slater, Jon Favreau, David Spade, and Adam Carolla. We did segments on Shaun White's twenty-first birthday party in Las Vegas (shredordie.com/video/dissent-tv-tony-and-shaun), and on Tommy Carroll, a blind skater from Illinois (shredordie.com/video/dissent-tv-tony-with-blind-1).

We've also done a few in-house "challenges," in which we bring in skaters of all levels, beginners to pros, to try something new and scary. The first one was simple: Three guys who barely skated competed for $1,000 cash by trying to drop in on the giant vert ramp in our warehouse (shredordie.com/video/1000-vert-drop). All they had to do was make the drop, roll across the ramp, and climb out on the other side. The U-shaped ramp is 13 feet high, with two feet of vertical at the top. Most people don't realize how intimidating that is for the average skater, because they only see pros ride the thing. I enjoyed watching the novice skaters edge up to the coping and look over, then inch by inch build up the nerve to take the plunge. Two of them made it on the third try, and split the cash.

For the next challenge, we set up the HuckJam's full loop in the parking lot outside our building and invited six skaters to give it a go. That one resulted in some hilarious near-death slams (shredordie. com/video/the-loop-challenge-2008). Two guys actually pulled it off: Alex Chalmers and Josh Borden.

In August 2009, we hosted our first huge online skate contest, called "Gear 4 a Year," in which we invited amateur skaters to upload video of themselves. The winner would receive a year's worth of skate-related products (from Foundation Skateboards, Silver trucks, Pig Wheels, Quiksilver clothes, Etnies shoes, and Nixon watches), guaranteed coverage in *The Skateboard Mag*, and automatic entry into the prestigious Tampa skate contest. The winner, Mike Thompson, didn't even know his friend had edited and posted the video until he'd been named a finalist (shredordie.com/video/video/listForCont ributor?screenName=2ceol9y3qchu8).

Some of the stuff we do on shredordie.com is more about laughing than shredding. On our "Free Lunch" channel, we take athletes out to lunch and try to make them as uncomfortable as possible. Dennis McCoy, the BMX legend, had just come out of surgery and arrived for an interview still woozy from anesthesia. His free lunch came back up. That was a popular video (shredordie.com/video/free-lunch-with-dennis-mccoy).

One of my favorite original shredordie.com shorts was made by vert skater Jesse Fritsch, BMXer Mike "Rooftop" Escamilla, and my hilarious nephew John Dale during the 2010 Gumball rally. Gumball is a car freak's decadent wet dream. Rich guys and celebrities from all over the world gather in Europe to drive ridiculously expensive cars (Ferrari's 612 Scaglietti, Bentley, Rolls-Royce Phantom, Aston-Martin DB9, Mercedes-Benz ML63 AMG, and more) in a big convoy from country to country. I've done it a few times as a special guest (meaning I agree to do press in exchange for a waived entry fee).

In 2010, we drove from London to Copenhagen, then flew to Boston to continue the race in the cars, which had been flown from Copenhagen to Maine. The organizers chartered a flight for most of the participants, and John, Jesse, and Rooftop persuaded pretty much everyone on the plane to join in making a mock music video to Bonnie Tyler's "Total Eclipse of the Heart." (The song request came from the rapper Xzibit, of all people.) Rappers, actors, tattooed DJs—all melodramatically mouth one of the goofiest power ballads ever written. Best scene: Xzibit singing, "Every now and then I get a little bit helpless and I'm lying like a child in your arms," while John tenderly hugs him (shredordie.com/video/gumball-2010-part-3-total-1).

That one went viral.

Unheard Music

In 2004, Steven Van Zandt came to our HuckJam arena show with a producer named Scott Greenstein. "Little Steven," as he's known, is a guitar player in Bruce Springsteen's E Street Band, but I knew him best for his role as Silvio Dante on *The Sopranos*. They came to ask if I'd be interested in hosting a weekly music and talk show on the satellite radio station, Sirius. Little Steven is a huge fan and supporter of underground music, and their enthusiasm for this new, uncensored, subscription-based radio format was infectious. Sirius eventually signed up Howard Stern, the superstar of raunchy radio, and their subscription base grew exponentially in a very short time.

The idea was to have me do a weekly, one-hour show in which I'd get to play music I liked and banter with my friends in the action-sports world. It would air on their punk rock channel, called Faction. They said they'd even build me a studio in my existing office building. The deal included stock options, and it sounded like fun, so I signed on. We decided to call it "Demolition Radio."

The executives at Sirius liked that I wanted to do shows live from my office, in the same building where I keep the HuckJam ramp assembled. That way, any skaters or BMXers who happened to drop by when we were on the air could join the show.

For a cast, I turned to two old friends, Jesse Fritsch and Jason Ellis. Both of them skate vert, play (or have played) in punk bands, and know how to make me laugh. In fact, Jason was so good on the air that Sirius soon gave him his own talk show. Now he's on five days a week and is one of Sirius's biggest stars. I replaced Jason with my nephew, John Dale, a budding stand-up comedian who's starred in videos on funnyordie.com and shredordie.com.

Our show has been fun and comfortable from the start. A lot of famous action-sports athletes have popped in, sometimes still sweating from their skate sessions: Shaun White, Bob Burnquist, Bucky Lasek, Andy Macdonald, Pierre Luc Gagnon, Kevin Robinson, Simon Tabron, and Dennis McCoy. We've also had on-the-air visits from Miley Cyrus, Elle Macpherson, Johnny Knoxville, Tom Green, Jon Favreau, and Reverend Run from Run-DMC.

Will Pendarvis from Sirius (which has since merged with its former rival, XM) has been my producer the whole time, helping to bridge the gap between the network's corporate office and all things Tony Hawk. He also makes sure we're geared up to record the show remotely when I'm on the road—which happens a lot. We've broadcast from trade shows like E3, the holy grail of video game conventions, and from the HuckJam and skatepark tours.

One of the most telling examples of the power of new media is that once I tweet that "Demolition Radio" is on the air, our phones light up with people calling in from all over the world—some of whom have told us they don't subscribe to Sirius/XM. Thanks to Twitter, I now have fans calling in to be on a live radio show they can't even hear.

10

HOW TO NEVER GET A MOVIE MADE

Hollywood will break your heart, or at least piss you off

I know for sure that there are a couple of things I do better than most people. One of them is ride a skateboard. The other is take meetings for movies that never get made. I've been doing it for decades, and I've become an expert at it.

Here's a Hollywood heartbreaker: In 2003, I got asked to star in a follow-up to the Warner Brothers hit movie *Space Jam*, which had teamed a real-life Michael Jordan with WB's Looney Tunes cartoon characters. This one would be titled *Skate Jam*. I'd be the featured human, acting alongside such two-dimensional icons as Bugs Bunny and Daffy Duck. I don't remember exactly how many times we met, but I do recall that the group pitching the project brought a lot of energy to every meeting. They set up storyboards illustrating the action-packed plot, and even had a cartoon-voice actor read lines from proposed scenes.

When it came time to have our last big meeting to finalize the deal, I was already scheduled to fly from Los Angeles to Australia, so they met me for dinner at that big tower-top restaurant at LAX. Everyone, including the WB contingent, was giddy with optimism. By then, they had the whole story fleshed out, and I liked what I heard. When the meal ended and we all shook hands, everyone was confident that we had the green light. As my agent walked with me toward the terminal, he claimed that the studio planned to offer me at least $1 million. I laughed all the way to Australia.

Unfortunately, the final decision on whether to go ahead with *Skate Jam* hinged on the success of another semi-sequel to *Space Jam*, called *Back in Action*, which turned out to be a relative flop.

I never even received a follow-up call.

Supreme Existential Strangeness

Because my career as a professional skater has continued after I stopped competing, I'm not one of those retired athletes who'd kill to be in a movie or to have his life story told. In fact, sometimes my existing ventures get in the way of Hollywood deals.

Let me illustrate that point with another cinematic tragedy: In 2001, my agent set me up with a producer who wanted to make a film based on my life story. The producer worked with Buena Vista, which was the distribution arm of Disney. Disney co-owned ESPN, which put on the X Games and thus owned rights to the footage of my first 900. It was all neatly linked.

The producer had read my autobiography, had watched the X Games replays, and was buzzing with enthusiasm. He envisioned the film opening with actual footage from the day I made that first 900, then freezing on a close-up of my face just before I dropped in for the successful run. Fade to a child actor playing me on a bench at a Little League game, trying to muster up the courage to tell my dad (who coached my team and ran the league) that I wanted to quit baseball and focus on skateboarding. All of that was true, so it sounded good to me. The best part was that I wouldn't have to do any acting. They'd have the "real" me through the X Games footage and then use actors of various ages to play the young me through the years.

Of course, we had many meetings. They even hired a screenwriter, who came to my office and pored over old photos, news clips, and memorabilia. I could tell that the writer was going to take some literary license with the facts—consolidated storylines, inflated drama, that kind of thing—but it wasn't enough to scare me away. I remember we actually had discussions about what advice I'd give the actor during scenes involving my first sexual encounter—a concept of supreme existential strangeness that I couldn't possibly have imagined back in high school when the encounter actually happened ... back when I used to get routinely ridiculed for riding a skateboard.

The whole idea of an autobiographic feature film was almost too much to consider, and I refused to discuss casting (Who would play my mother? My girlfriend? The 12-year-old me?) until I knew such decisions were imminent.

Everyone said it was a no-miss. Skateboarding and other action sports were just starting to take off, and Disney/ESPN was eager to give the category (and thus the X Games) a boost with this movie.

While the writer researched my most embarrassing adolescent anecdotes, my film agent at William Morris worked on hammering out the Disney contract. Problems arose when they started talking about the possibility of creating and selling consumer products related to the movie. Merchandising, as it's called, was practically invented by Disney; they've been doing it since 1929, when Mickey Mouse's image first appeared on a children's writing tablet. So they like to have control over licensing outside products. I couldn't see how a biopic would have much merchandising potential, but it turned out to be a major snag. I couldn't grant them licensing rights in categories that already had products with my name on them, like apparel, sporting goods, and some toys. I knew the project was in trouble when I heard both sides were arguing about coffee mugs.

Needless to say, that movie never got made, either.

A similar conflict scuttled an idea for a Saturday morning cartoon series that my agent brought to the table in 2004. It would be for young boys, and have my name on it. The proposal came from a production company that had produced some successful direct-to-DVD movies based on some very popular toy brands. I liked their idea, but, again, we clashed over licensing rights.

Not surprisingly, the biggest source of revenue for most televised cartoon shows comes from consumer products that get sold around the brand: SpongeBob SquarePants pajamas, Yo Gabba Gabba sippy cups, that kind of thing. Also, good animation is expensive. Consequently, the producer wanted to use the revenue from merchandise sales to cover the costs of production, estimated at $500,000 or more per episode. I would have been cool with figuring out a revenue-sharing

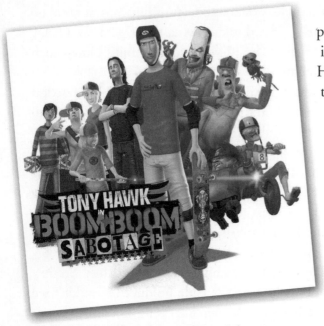

Although the sales of Boom Boom Sabotage were not what we hoped for, the creative work was amazing. Here is the animated "me" along with the rest of the characters.
Courtesy of © Rainmaker Entertainment Inc.®

deal for the sale of products—but they insisted that "Tony Hawk" had to be in the show's title and thus would be on the merchandise, and that (again) would create too many conflicts with my existing licensing business.

After a long series of less-than-pleasant negotiations, we killed the series idea and instead agreed to produce an animated, direct-to-DVD movie based on my Boom Boom HuckJam tour. This also fulfilled a contractual obligation that would have been costly to escape from. Sales weren't great, but the final product was much better than I'd expected, especially in light of all the conflict leading up to it.

False Promises, Fast Cars

All of this frustration has taught me a couple of lessons.

First, never bank on anything that has to do with Hollywood. A movie can be hours away from actual production, with actors hired and a crew assembled, and someone at the top might still pull the plug. So if a movie mogul shakes your hand and looks you in the eye and promises that this film you've been pitching is *definitely* going to be made, don't run out and buy a Lamborghini just yet.

Second, despite the limited chance for success, take all the meetings you can with legitimate filmmakers, and remain polite (unless you're dealing with a certified asshole), because the film industry is all about connections and unburned bridges

For example, not long after the Buena Vista deal fell through, my agent set up a meeting with Stacey Snider, longtime chairman of Universal Studios. Stacey had an impeccable reputation. She'd been instrumental in developing such hit films as *Erin Brockovich*, *The Fast and the Furious*, and *The Mummy* movies. (She eventually left Universal to head up DreamWorks.)

Stacey seemed genuinely interested in developing a project for both me and my production company, 900 Films. She suggested we meet with screenwriter Gary Scott Thompson, who'd just written Universal's big hit, *The Fast and the Furious*, starring Vin Diesel. Over lunch, Gary told us he was looking to do something with action

I had a cameo as an astronaut in *The Lords of Dogtown*. Lhotse had a smaller cameo as a NASA publicist.

sports. Soon, he began coming up with concepts for a film. But again, as is so often the case in Hollywood, Gary got sidetracked by other projects. Eventually, NBC picked up his television show *Las Vegas*, and nothing ever came of our meetings with him.

However, that connection eventually led us to the director of *The Fast and the Furious*, Rob Cohen, who was working on another Vin Diesel action feature called *xXx*. Cohen was interested in working with 900 Films because the movie was about a rebellious action-sports star who gets recruited by the National Security Agency to infiltrate a group of terrorists. Cohen ended up using several well-known skateboarders, BMXers, and motocross riders as stunt men, extras, and bit players. He also hired 900 Films' best cameraman, Matt Goodman, to shoot the snowboarding and other stunt sequences.

This, in turn, led Matt to shoot all of the main action for a terribly cheesy movie about skating called *Grind* (which I declined to be in after reading the script). The movie was overwhelmingly panned, although several reviews noted that the film's only bright spot was Matt's action footage. I still don't understand how so many bad ideas get made into films while good ones get quashed.

Tom Cruise Gets Mushy

These days, through my company 900 Films, I'm more interested in the production side of the movie business. I've been especially intrigued by a project we began pitching a few years ago in which we'd use dazzling 3-D technology to film original stunts by top athletes in four sports: surfing, skateboarding, BMX, and motocross. We'd document each stunt's entire process, from inception to execution, in exotic locations. Sort of *The Endless Summer* meets *Road Trip*, in 3-D.

We started getting interest from a few studios after we aligned with Brett Morgen, director of such acclaimed documentaries as *The Kid Stays in the Picture*, *On the Ropes*, and *Chicago 10*. As an accomplished documentarian, Brett was an expert at weaving together strong narratives out of existing footage—and this time the footage was guaranteed to be mind-blowing. At one point, we had Kelly Slater, Shaun White, and Mat Hoffman in the main cast. As the project started to build a little buzz, our agent hinted that we might even luck into the best possible scenario: a bidding war.

The big moment came when Brett and I got summoned to have dinner with Tom Cruise, who'd just become head of MGM's newly resurrected studio United Artists. The meeting was to take place at his house. I had no idea what to expect, but it seemed like a good sign. We drove to an inconspicuous gate off of Sunset Boulevard, then made our way to a guest house/screening room. Tom arrived a little late because he was out flying with his kids. We were joined at dinner by Paula Wagner (his UA partner), his agent, and the agent representing Brett and me.

Tom told us he knew our world because he used to ride his BMX bike down a steep hill and fly off a launch ramp at the bottom. Paula was shocked, and kept saying things like "Oh my gawwwwd, Tom! You're craaaaazy!"

The weirdest part was that Tom's sister would come in periodically and hand him a note, which he'd share with us. First note: His wife had just landed in New Orleans. Second note: She was at the hotel. Tom picked up a nearby house phone and proceeded to have the mushiest oh-baby-I-love-you-miss-you-so-much-have-good-dreams goo-goo conversation I've ever witnessed. It was one of the most awkward things I've ever had to sit through. In the end, though, he redeemed himself in my eyes when it became clear that he's a good father who genuinely loves his kids. And his kids were extremely courteous and respectful, so I'll cut the man some slack.

Anyway, the pitch didn't go well. Tom grilled us about very specific filmmaking details, like what kind of lenses and camera mounts we'd use to capture the action. Most of all, though, he wanted to know about the storyline, which we had always figured would unfold as the shooting progressed. It was, after all, a documentary. But he said he needed a dramatic arc that he could "bring back to my people."

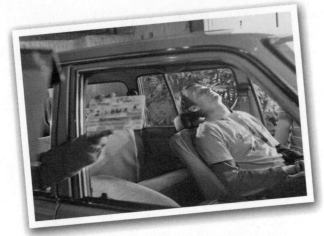

Here I am, dead, on the set of *CSI: Miami*. Action!

I didn't understand. Hadn't we reached the top? Didn't the buck stop here? Didn't *he* have the power to give the green light? We held strong, trying to give reassuring answers without making false promises. Apparently it wasn't enough. We never heard back.

Going Indie

Although I've all but given up on doing something with a big studio, I still hope to create something that Hollywood will be interested in. Our current plan is to do it from the bottom up, through our website shredordie.com, which aggregates amateur and semiprofessional action-sports video shorts. We're now pitching an alt-sports version of the HBO series *Funny or Die Presents*, which is a spinoff of shredordie.com's sister website funnyordie.com.

A lot of the best stuff on shredordie.com was produced quickly and cheaply by the nimble crew at 900 Films, and I'm convinced that if we can get the right network execs to just look at the footage, they'll bite. The best thing about this idea is that we don't have to wait for a studio to give the green light before we're allowed to turn on a camera. It's really satisfying when one of my talented friends comes up with a good idea for a short video, and within days it gets shot, edited, and posted online. No storyboards, no casting calls, no sippy cups, no lunatic moguls.

And no meetings.

11

STINKY DIAPERS IN FIRST CLASS

How to balance travel and family: bring 'em

few years ago, when my youngest son Keegan was in preschool, the teachers asked the students in his class to describe the kind of work their fathers did. The teachers then wrote the responses on paper and pinned them to the classroom wall. Most of their quotes were cute: "My dad sells money," and "My dad figures stuff out."

Here's what Keegan said about me: "I've never seen my dad do work."

I suppose that shouldn't have come as a surprise, considering that I make my living doing something that my sons see as fun and that I obviously enjoy. Only occasionally—when a demo ramp sucks, for example, or I have to perform with a tweaked ankle— does skateboarding itself feel like "work."

I'm acutely aware that I've been very, very lucky in my career, and

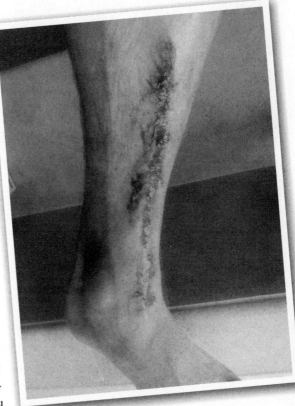

that much of my success has to do with being at the right place at the right time. And in recent years, after traveling to places like Sierra Leone and Cambodia, I've grown increasingly grateful that I don't have to sort trash or sell rags to feed my family. There are 12-year-olds mining diamonds in West Africa for pennies a day; I've made millions by riding a skateboard. It's one of those cosmic absurdities, and I try hard not to lose sight of it.

So while I don't have to "do work," as Keegan put it, I have tried to develop a work ethic. For example, if I promise to make an appearance or attend a meeting, I do everything in my power to get there on time and stick with the schedule. Nothing pisses off fans (or stresses event organizers) more than when a celebrity arrives late or leaves early. Most of the actual "work" I do requires me to travel—a lot. I'm on the road 100 to 150 days a year;

I've been a member of United Airlines' 1K Club (meaning I've flown 100,000 miles per year) for nearly 10 years in a row. I don't mind being on the road, especially with my skater friends, but I also love being home with my four kids.

I could write a long essay about the intricate dance that's required to create a nominally stable domestic life when your job requires you to be gone half of the year. Instead, I thought it best to illustrate the concept with excerpts from various journals and blogs I've kept in recent years.

April 12–15, 2004
Sport for Good Foundation, Sierra Leone, West Africa

As an official member of the Laureus World Sports Academy, I was asked to visit one of the Sport for Good Foundation (Laureus's primary charity) projects to see first hand their efforts to offer sports and other activities to needy youth in places like India, Brazil, and China.

The call finally came for me to visit a project in Sierra Leone. I only knew the country from the civil war it fought for years, and the atrocities that were occasionally covered in the news.

In Sierra Leone, Laureus supports a program called Right to Play (RTP), which gives traumatized children a chance to simply be kids again. The program has trained about 400 local volunteers to organize games and leagues with equipment provided by the charity. So far, about 5,000 Sierra Leone teenagers have joined in RTP sporting events. A lot of these kids had been forced into combat, labor camps,

and sexual slavery during the country's dark war-torn years. They're just now learning to do the things that kids are supposed to do, like playing soccer or volleyball or Frisbee.

It took Lhotse and me 30 hours to get from San Diego to Freetown, Sierra Leone. In my wildest dreams, I never imagined that

I would end up in a place like this just from riding a skateboard. Children were everywhere: in the gutted and burned houses, on the streets, in the diamond mines (which we could see from the road), and at the multitude of streetfront retail stands. Most wore torn clothes. Few had shoes.

The first thing I noticed as we pulled up to the RTP site was the abundance of happy faces on all the kids, regardless of age. And they were some of the most well-behaved and engaged kids I have ever seen playing together. They waited for the coaches' instructions and made the most of whatever game they happened to be playing. It was a far cry from the too-cool-for-school kids that I'm used to seeing on playgrounds back home. I jumped in, joining the limbo line and losing at the soccer dribbling races. One of the best moments came when Lhotse showed some of the kids the video she'd shot of them and they freaked.

At the next site we visited, volleyball was obviously the most popular activity. There was a demolished school nearby where I found just enough intact concrete to skate. As I wove around broken cement and exposed dirt, the locals were perplexed by this "roller boogie," as they called it. It was kind of like traveling from the future to show what will be possible, and quickly leaving before anyone has a chance to figure it out.

Later that day, at a playground, we met a girl who appeared to be about 12 years old and pregnant. She was knitting a baby pouch for her future newborn.

It was unnerving— not because of the babies-having-babies aspect, but because everyone took it as normal. We also saw three- and four-year-olds with babies strapped to their back— toddlers caring for infants. I can't even get my five-year-old son Spencer to look after his favorite Hot Wheels car, let alone his younger brother.

Back at the hotel, drained, we fell right asleep. When I woke up for dinner, I missed my boys more than ever.

The next morning, all the RTP volunteers gathered in the town's only real soccer field for a full day of activities involving about 500 kids. Later, we went to the certificate presentation and listened to some long-winded speeches. When it was my turn to talk, I pledged to spread the word about the good work being done there by the Sport for Good and Right to Play projects, and to help raise more funds for their programs. I'd feel like I accomplished something if my visit opened some eyes and more kids got soccer balls in the process. They're kids, after all, and they just want to play.

July 1–7, 2004

Adio Tour, England

I was skeptical about going on a week-long core tour (meaning that it would be mostly street), but my son Riley was out of school for the summer and it was time to get back into skatepark mode. We did a total of three demos over the course of six days, but most of our time was spent driving between stops. Overall, it was a good trip. Riley and his friend Shaun Stulz were the

Riley Hawk and Shaun Stulz.

highlights of each demo, getting just as tech as some of the pros and inspiring the younger skaters in attendance. Here are some of the highlights (and lowlights):

- Riley's video camera being stolen from him by some thug kids while he was passing a bus stop in London. I was across the street when it happened. They now possess an NTSC camera that they can't charge and can't play on their televisions. Good luck, guys.
- The genuine appreciation of the crowds in England. I have never heard such applause for basic tricks.
- If an organizer told us that a place was 20 minutes away, it was an hour. If they said it was an hour away, then it was three. This means that we were consistently late for autograph sessions or demos, and we regularly checked into hotels between 2:00 and 4:00 A.M.

- *Chappelle's Show* (Season 1) on DVD made the drives much easier.
- Autograph sessions that seemed more important to the crowds than live skating (and lasted longer than any of the demos).

- Sightseeing in London. "Look, kids, Big Ben! The House of Parliament!" That was the extent of our excursions.
- Spending July 4 in the land that we celebrate getting away from. For some reason, we weren't invited to any cookouts or fireworks displays.
- Being back on a real skate tour after a long hiatus and getting to enjoy it through the eyes of my son.

August 27–29, 2004
MTV Video Music Awards, Miami, Florida

Amid the hip-hop decadence and VIP parties, I recall the following:

- Presenting the best new artist award with Ashlee Simpson, during which the stage was "transformed" into a skatepark and I joined in a live demo.
- Walking by all of the A-list celebs in the front row (including Puffy and Jay-Z), and realizing that I was still wearing my helmet. *Whassup, cuz? I'm chillin'.*

- While we sat in the audience during the televised ceremony, a production assistant came over and told me that I would be presenting the award for Best Video Game Soundtrack in the next segment. I said that there must be some mistake, that our game was nominated for that award and I'd yet to see a script for the presentation. She went away flustered and I sat there wondering what to do. She came back soon after and corrected herself: I was going to *win* that award in the next segment. Suddenly I found myself on stage with Good Charlotte and D12 making an acceptance speech with Bam Margera, for a *music* award. And you may ask yourself: "Well, how did I get here?"

October 2, 2004
Andre Agassi's Grand Slam for Children, Las Vegas, Nevada

My friend Robert invited me to be his guest at Andre Agassi's annual charity event, heralded as one of the most consistently successful live fundraisers. I thought it would be good to check it out, lend my support, and possibly learn a few things that could help with our first THF fundraiser (happening the very next day). All of the raised money goes toward Andre's charity: a school for underprivileged children located in the outskirts of Vegas. I believe they have raised over $50 million so far, so the school is thriving. There are plans to expand it into a college and take the idea to other cities as well.

The main draw for the Agassi event is live entertainment, and this year was no exception. Robin Williams, Faith Hill, John Mayer, and Ray Romano were all scheduled to appear, making the $20,000-per-table cost seem like an extravagant ticket price as opposed to a straight donation. The auction items were of the same caliber: private tennis lessons with Andre and Steffi Graf; a trip on a private jet to meet the First Lady for lunch; and other one-of-a-kind offers.

Andre asked me to get up and offer an auction item of my choice, so I went on stage and came up with a private demo for five to be held at our new office (on the BBHJ ramp), with catering by

McDonald's. A bidding began between two high-roller philanthropists, so I ended up offering two such demos—which raised the total to six figures. I never imagined that a few McTwists and some Happy Meals would be worth that much.

October 3, 2004

Stand Up for Skateparks Fundraiser, Studio City, California

Today we held our first fundraiser for the Tony Hawk Foundation at the Pinz Bowling Alley in Studio City. We wanted to make sure that there was plenty for kids to do, but also a constant schedule of live entertainment. Having David Spade commit to doing a small routine was the catalyst for getting us going in full gear. Not long after we set the date, Blink-182 joined the roster, and things snowballed from there. The setting was Pinz Bowling Alley in Studio City, with skating and playthings

Benecio del Toro and me.

in the parking lot and comedy and music inside. And if someone managed to get bored, they could always bowl.

Besides the multitude of kids' activities (and food) outside, our plan was to have a skate and BMX demo, a live auction, comedy, and, finally, music. Todd Glass opened for Spade, and Tom Green introduced me when I got up to explain our foundation's mission and to summarize the auction items. Our auction items were unique: a private surf lesson with Kelly Slater; a private skate demo with yours truly; a Hawaiian vacation in a private villa; and a guitar autographed by Blink. The last item was donated by Bobby Kotick (CEO of Activision), who bought it at another fundraiser, and was kind enough to re-gift it. Mat Hoffman donated the bike he had just ridden in our outdoor demo.

The auction went relatively well, but it was hard for me to get excited about items going for $2,000 to $5,000 after seeing the extravagance of the Agassi event. In the end, we raised nearly $500,000, so I have no complaints. Pamela Anderson bought

Spencer with Pamela Anderson.

Mat Hoffman's bike for $6,000, after which Mat suggested that she put brakes on it. She also paid $5,000 for a date with Spade. David said he looked forward to taking her to Sizzler. Ryan Sheckler bought the Blink guitar for $4,000.

The only sad face I saw the whole day was my son Spencer, after he ran out of quarters in the arcade—a tragedy quickly remedied by his aunt and grandma.

April 22–24, 2005

Black Pearl Skatepark Grand Opening, Grand Cayman, Cayman Islands

My invitation to the opening of the world's biggest skatepark had been postponed many times due to construction delays and hurricane damage. We were invited to visit the 60,000-square-foot park more as a vacation than an obligation (translation: free travel, no pay). I invited an eclectic skate crew: me, Riley, Shaun Stulz, Steve Nesser, Mike Vallely, Kevin Staab, Alex Chalmers, and our respective wives, fiancées, and girlfriends.

The first thing we noticed was that Hurricane Ivan had hit this remote island like a big, bad bomb. Trees were uprooted, boats were still lying where they'd been pushed ashore, and the majority of dwellings were in the process of being rebuilt. Fortunately, most of our hotel was open and the beach water out front was bluer than I had ever seen anywhere.

Our first outing was a luxury boat tour. We went snorkeling on the outer reef and then on to one of Cayman's landmark tourist spots, Stingray City. Hordes of stingrays flock and swim in, out, and around the legs of screeching landlubbers, who feed them nuggets of sliced squid. The only rules: don't pet their backs and don't step on them, which become increasingly difficult to follow once the rays start swarming. It's almost overwhelming to have so many potentially dangerous animals boldly brushing up against your body. Even Riley got off the boat and mingled with the locals for a while, until one glided across his legs and he quickly jumped on my back.

The next day, we checked out the skatepark, which is monstrous in every way. It appears to go on forever, and every visible wall looks to be at least 10 feet high. The place offers an amazing mass of transitions, but it would be better explored over a week instead of one day.

Demo day: It was crowded, but not nearly the thousands we'd been warned about. It was hard doing a demo in such an expansive park. I'd love to go back and explore all of it without the pressure of a crowd watching.

After the demo, we headed back to our hotel for stereotypical Cayman activities: lying on the beach, riding Jet Skis, and ordering drinks. We even caught a glimpse of Iggy Pop doing the same thing by the pool, smashing every misconception I had about this place. It's not lawyers and Mafiosos hiding money and living in excess. It's more about families, pro skaters, and rockers getting away for some sun and relaxation.

June 10–12, 2005

Disneyland, Vegas, Arkansas, Home, Spokane, Various Events

My life is weird. In the past few days, I've introduced Arnold Schwarzenegger at an event, taken my kids to Disneyland, been Punk'd, played in a high-roller poker tournament in Vegas, helped design a backyard skatepark for the TV show *Extreme Makeover: Home Edition*, and spent exactly eight hours at home getting ready for this summer's Boom Boom HuckJam tour. Some highlights:

- Governor Schwarzenegger's office prepared my speech for an event at Disneyland where I was supposed to introduce him so he could announce the formation of something called the California Governor's Council on Physical Fitness and Sports. I put it in my own words and sent it back. They said I wasn't allowed to make changes to my own speech. So I said, "No thanks, I'd rather not do it." They said they'd look at it and get back to me. They approved my words.
- I skated up to the podium and introduced the Governator while standing next to Michelle Kwan and Jack LaLanne, fellow members of the new fitness council.

- Riley Punk'd me. That's all I'm allowed to say until MTV airs the show.
- Met the following people at the Wynn hotel in Vegas: Wayne Gretzky, Matt Damon, and Steve Wynn. I also met multibillionaire Warren Buffett as we sat down to a lavish dinner. There was lobster, caviar, fancy French dishes, and Dom Perignon. Warren had chicken fingers and a Coke.
- Lost miserably in the Netjets Poker tournament. Nobody fell for my bluffs. I officially suck at poker. The guy who placed third won a Maserati. A Maserati! For third!
- Got some redemption at the blackjack table with my lucky Lhotse sitting anchor.
- Flew from Vegas to Fort Smith, Arkansas, to help Ty of *Extreme Makeover: Home Edition* design a backyard mini-ramp for a lucky family there. Lhotse and I were in Arkansas for a total of three hours.
- Got home in time to pack two giant bags for the BBHJ tour and sleep for four hours.
- Arrived in Spokane for the first BBHJ show and immediately went to test our new Bigass Ramp: a 44-foot drop to a 40-foot gap to a 20-foot quarterpipe. It was one of the scariest things I've ever done.
- After six flights and three hotels in three days, we're finally settled in Spokane. Daily rehearsals until our first show on 6/17. It's good to be back somewhere familiar: on tour.

July 8–31, 2005

Boom Boom HuckJam Tour, Home, DC, MO, IA, MN, WI, MI, OH, NJ, PA, Toronto, NY, MA

I am officially over sleeping on a bus and waking up in a different city and checking into hotels only to shower and change clothes. The shows were a blast, though. Some high- and lowlights from our whirlwind adventures:

- I made a surprise visit to the GreenSkateLab skatepark in DC—one of the parks that received a grant from the TH Foundation. I did an invert on the only vert wall in the deep end and managed to hang up on the way in, sending me straight to the flat on my hip and shoulder. It hurt a lot, and the next four shows were a lesson in pain tolerance.

- Mat Hoffman took the worst slam I have ever seen live. He locked up on his sprocket coming in from a 10-foot air and took the

handlebars to his chest before going straight to his head on the flat. I was convinced he had a concussion and internal damage and was done for the tour. But backstage during intermission he took the oxygen mask off and asked if his bike was okay, and then went back out to ride, despite newly bruised ribs and giant, fresh contusions on his knees. Mat Hoffman is the toughest and most dedicated athlete in the world.

- Riley came out for some shows and learned the art of design-bleaching shirts from Drake. He smelled like ammonia for days.

- Went home for one night between Milwaukee and Detroit. Had a birthday party for Keegan, washed some clothes, recorded a radio show, and headed back to the airport. Our flight was canceled, so we had to wait around LAX for nearly eight hours and catch a red-eye to Detroit to make our show there the next day. This jet-set lifestyle is not so glamorous sometimes.

- Just when my hip was feeling better, I fell on it in the exact same place, right at the beginning of a four-show stretch. But I still don't hold a candle to what Mat must go through all the time.

- Jon Bon Jovi came to our NJ show with his family. As a tribute, we played "Bad Medicine" during the jam.

- Rune Glifberg started pulling 360s over the jump near the end of the tour, but over-rotated during practice in Philly and went down hard. He bruised his lung, ribs, shoulder, hip, elbow, and probably other spots he didn't mention. He didn't skate the rest of the shows but stayed on tour to keep our spirits high.

- Kevin Robinson and I visited wounded troops in DC. These guys have heart-wrenching stories of losing limbs (and buddies) in battle, mostly during their time in Iraq. They are profiles in courage and make my injuries (and even Mat's) look like minor scratches in comparison.

September 9–18, 2005

Secret Skatepark Tour, OR, MT, IN, Cayman Islands, GA

I presented the idea to Activision to do another secret skatepark tour, this time in conjunction with the

release of *Tony Hawk's American Wasteland* (*THAW*), and they were down to support it. The only stipulation was to include as many riders from the video game as possible, and to have playable demos of *THAW* at each stop. I handpicked each park based on quality, location, and whether we donated money to the project through the Tony Hawk Foundation.

The lineup changed along the way, but at one point we had the following group: Bam, Bob Burnquist, Mike Vallely, Daewon Song, Ryan Sheckler, Steve Nesser, Shaun Stulz, and Rick

Thorne. People freaked when we showed up to parks in places like Grants Pass, Oregon, and Fort Wayne, Indiana. We got the surprise factor that I'd hoped to achieve with our original secret tour (but never seemed to catch on video). Some highlights:

- Showing up to Great Falls, Montana, an hour before dark and watching the crowd grow like wildfire once word spread that we were there. It was such a scene that the cops started issuing tickets to people (including our tour manager) not wearing helmets. Mike V. and I confronted one overzealous officer about humiliating kids by putting them in the back of the cop car while writing their tickets. Not surprisingly, this exchange did not go well and ended with Mike and me leaving the park in protest while hundreds of kids booed the cops. Within minutes, four more patrol cars showed up, and a no-helmet ticketing frenzy ensued. Why provide a facility to keep kids from skating on the streets if you're just going to hassle them at that very place? Fish in a barrel, I suppose.
- Bam coming along on a skate-only trip. He's been so overwhelmed with his MTV show and various movie projects that he hasn't had time to focus on his skating much. He was ripping by the end.
- Watching every-one's reactions when they first encountered stingrays in Cayman. It trans-formed a group of scarred and tattooed skaters into shrieking kids, jumping out of waist-deep water in fits of fright and delight.

Mike V. and me.

- Going to a middle school in Helena, Montana, and announcing that we would be at the skatepark down the street after school, then skating through the gym to the surprise of the P.E. students. The park was *packed* once the bell rang.
- Turning our demo in Athens, Georgia, into a last-minute fund-raiser for Katrina victims. There was no entry fee, but spectators were encouraged to make a $10 donation, and all concession proceeds went to the fund. Marriott agreed to match any money raised. Total take: about $30,000.

August–November 2007
France, Germany, NYC, NC, LA, SF

I spent my last summer days hanging out with the kids and killing myself for *The Beginning*, our new Birdhouse video. The alley-oop backside ollie over a 20-foot channel was my favorite trick that happened spontaneously. The premiere happened less than a week after I got my last few tricks. The most exciting aspect of the video for me is that Riley has his own legitimate part and his stuff is *good*. It's been nine years since we released a video. Here's what else happened:

- Over the course of 10 days, I traveled to NYC twice to do a mélange of TV shows and appearances: *TRL*, MSNBC, *Fox & Friends*, ESPN, Yahoo!, Fuse, *The Naked Brothers Band*, a Laureus dinner, and an appearance for Steiner Sports. At least there's plenty of good food in Manhattan to enjoy between obligations.

- Had Thanksgiving at my brother's house in Half Moon Bay, just south of San Francisco. We hired a boat to check out Maverick's, the big-wave spot, which was breaking thanks to a rare swell. Our skipper put us a little too close to the action, and we barely made it over the shoulder of one of the biggest waves of the day. It felt like we dropped 40 feet on the way down the back. My mom was on the tip of the bow. She thought it was fun.

December 2007–February 2008
Compton, Vegas, Woodward, Hawaii, Whistler, LA

Every time I feel like things are starting to slow down, they blow up again. The holidays were no exception. My wife and I found out we're having a baby, which will be my first girl! This was not spontaneous or romantic, but the fruit of a full year of fertility treatments, dozens of shots in her stomach and hips, hope, worry, and tireless disappointment. Modern medicine is amazing…and expensive. But it works! We can't wait for our June baby. Meanwhile, I've been skating nonstop. So has Riley; he's turned into an amazing street skater, better than I ever imagined. I hope he'll teach me switch flips soon. Here is what else I've been up to:

- Presented the City of Compton with the check for their skatepark during a city council meeting. I still can't believe we raised $60,000 in a matter of minutes at our last fundraiser.
- Attended the 2007 Spike Video Game Awards. I flew in, handed out an award, and flew home. I was in Vegas for only a few hours— a most uneventful trip to Sin City.
- Spent the New Year in Kauai with my family and the Underhills. It had been Ray's dream to take a helicopter tour in Hawaii and we made it happen. It rained most of the time, but it didn't stop our kids from surfing Hanalei every day. Kilauea is incredible even when it's pouring.

- Went to Whistler, BC, for one day at the request of Benji Weatherley for his film project. Rode powder all day with Todd Richards, Shane Dorian, Jake Burton, and Tosh Townend, then flew home the next morning.

- Mia Hamm Celebrity Soccer Challenge. Mia asked if I could join her cause to register potential bone marrow donors by playing in a soccer match with other celebrities and some soccer pros. I've never played a real game of soccer in my life, so it was intimidating to be out in front of thousands of people my first time on the pitch. It was more fun and way more work than I had assumed. Rivers Cuomo (of Weezer) was one of many on my team who took it seriously, but it seems that he takes *everything* seriously. The most rewarding aspect was seeing the donors and recipients meet (for the first time ever) during halftime.

March–June 2008
Russia, Japan, Vegas, Hospital!

It's been hard to keep a journal with things in a state of flux recently. It seems like we have been awaiting the arrival of our daughter for nearly two years (well, we have in some ways), and all plans were tentative until her arrival. Here is what happened during those last months of her incubation:

- Went to St. Petersburg, Russia, for the Laureus Awards. Lhotse and I were lucky to have Miki Vuckovich (head of the TH Foundation) as our tour guide. He lived in St. Pete during the oppressive years and was able to give us insight about many of the landmarks and customs. The most exciting part for me

was buying an Ushanka hat (with earflaps) and being offered cans of caviar by a street hustler. I wish we had time to skate, but we were there for only two nights.

- Took a family trip to Japan. It was something I always wanted to share with my mom, brother, and sisters since my first visit. It was fun to see their faces upon first seeing sushi and dried octopus at 7-Elevens, and to share barbequed squid-on-a-stick from a street vendor.

- The only downside was missing the Kids' Choice Awards and finding out too late that I'd won the award for favorite male athlete. But nothing will replace the memories of Kyoto and searching all day for the skatepark with Riley. It's not the destination, it's the journey that matters.

- Turned 40 in style with a *Big Lebowski* bowling bash in Las Vegas. Careful, man, there's a beverage here.

- On June 30, 2008, we welcomed Kadence into the world. My first daughter. She looks just like her beautiful mommy. Her brothers are very excited. Life will never be the same. I can't wait.

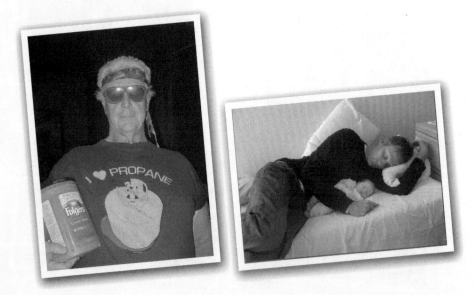

May 12–16, 2010
Woodward Skate Camp Opening, Beijing, China

The flight from SFO to Beijing had so many skaters on board it looked like a chartered jet. Who would summon such a crew across the world? Woodward Skate Camp and their first international installation: Woodward Beijing.

We landed 12 hours later and shuttled straight to the new facility, which is amazing: a full-size street course, three separate bowls connected by spines and wall rides, a foampit for launching, two mini-Megaramps, and two vert ramps. Jet lag was quickly forgotten. Curren Caples chose one of the biggest gaps in the place as his warmup while Riley, David Loy, and Aaron "Jaws" Homoki worked on their Megaramp tricks into the foam pit. After a couple hours of skating and delirious sweating, we went inside for a traditional Chinese buffet with dish names like "meat with pineapple" and "exploding goat."

Not long after, my two-year-old daughter passed out from exhaustion. The rest of us weren't far behind.

Day Two started at 3:30 A.M. with a tiny girl's voice calling, "Dada, Yo Gabba Gabba please." No use trying to explain the concept of jet lag to a two-year-old. After a short morning skate session, we took tours of Tiananmen Square and the Forbidden City, then headed to the Quiksilver store in Sanlitun. Quiksilver is doing a great job of importing the boardsports culture to China in a way that doesn't look too Western or far out. Still, people had no idea what to make of a grown American man skateboarding around the streets, especially when he puts his blond daughter on the front for rides along the walkways. They were also tripping on Kevin Staab's purple hair.

On Day Three, we visited the Great Wall, where vendors did everything they could to block our path in hopes of selling us T-shirts, chess sets, stamps, books, noodles, dried fruit, and cliché hats. The best sales tactic was to put a small Chinese flag in the hand of my daughter, who refused to let it go, giving me no choice but to pay for it. It wasn't until we were riding a chairlift to the top that we got a sense of how massive the Great Wall really is.

On the day of the grand opening, everything was scheduled down to five-minute intervals. The Chinese government (including a "Chairman of Extreme Sports") doesn't mess around when it comes to their time. It was a long day, with demos, speeches, cheerleaders, and a lunch featuring such delicacies as "fried sausage" and "chicken string." Many of us fell asleep by 7:00 P.M., only to be awakened an hour later by fireworks right next to the hotel. My daughter liked all of the colors but none of the noise. Now she wants me to go buy "more fire."

Tweets, 2009–2010

Dear Santa: I would once again like to have rock/punk/hip hop songs stuck in my head instead of Elmo melodies. Sincerely, Tony.

■ ■ ■

I just hid a skateboard between two trash cans at Abbey Road Studios. Go now.

■ ■ ■

Abbey Road has been found, so please stop lurking around there like a 5th Beatle.

■ ■ ■

Dear Kia: Including Muno & Sock Monkey in a commercial has added a very young female to your demographic. Expect her purchase in 16 years.

My daughter Kady.

■ ■ ■

Anyone out there connected with the A-Team movie? Looking for a PR or promo connection ...

■ ■ ■

The power of Twitter, exemplified: I hadn't secured a car for Gumball Rally as of today. A friend: "What about the A-Team van?" (cont'd).

■ ■ ■

"The movie is out soon. They might let you use it for promotion," I tweet; @iambenlyons responds with contact info at Fox.

■ ■ ■

Five hours later we secure the van (the ACTUAL movie prop). That JUST happened thanks to Natalie at Fox. I love it when a plan comes together.

■ ■ ■

Dear media outlets and event organizers: I am not your link to Shaun White. He will not magically appear in my presence. Sincerely, Tony.

■ ■ ■

My 10-year-old's review of an English park: "This is the sketchiest playground EVER! It's AWESOME!" Lack of liability laws = fun for kids.

■ ■ ■

When asked what tattoo he would ever consider getting, my 10-year-old paused & said: "The words 'Does this make me look fat?' on my belly."

■ ■ ■

Me to my ultra-finicky 11-yr-old: "What would it take to try new food?" Him: "What can I ask for?" Me: "Whatever." Him: "Half of California."

■ ■ ■

Waterboarding is so 2006. Getting kicked in the head by a squirming toddler all night is the new torture.

■ ■ ■

Kid at skatepark: "You met my grandma Karen one time! Do you remember her?" Me: "Not exactly, sorry." Him: "Was she wearing a pink shirt?"

■ ■ ■

Don't you hate it when a baby is loud & squirming an entire overseas flight? You could never be "those" people. We have become those people.

12

GIVING BACK

Family, friends, Regis, and a very smart fifth-grader help me build a charity

From: ▮▮▮▮▮▮▮
To: <TONY@CLUBTONYHAWK.COM>
Subject: your #1 fan and i mean it

Dear Tony Hawk,

I keep asking my dad if he can build me a little skatepark, but he's always like, "I'm too busy." There is a big skatepark here but there are a lot of big kids who swear and knock me over. So if you have any extra time, could you come to my house and build one with me?

I live in ▮▮▮▮ just off of ▮▮▮▮▮ ▮▮▮ on ▮▮ ▮ ▮▮▮▮▮ ▮▮. Get to ▮▮▮ and turn right on to ▮▮▮▮ and then turn left on ▮▮▮ ▮▮▮ then left on ▮▮▮▮▮ and its the ▮▮▮ house to your right. Got all that? Now Pleeeeeeeeeeeese come. I need to sk8 or I will die.

n 2001, I got invited to do a demo at the grand opening of a public skatepark near Chicago. The community that invited me was affluent—they could afford to fly in a celebrity skater from California as part of their opening-day fanfare. I arrived the day before the big event, and they asked if I wanted to ride the park that afternoon, alone. I jumped at the chance, figuring I'd give it a test run before I skated the place in front of a crowd.

The park, unfortunately, was a joke—a nonsensical arrangement of poorly constructed obstacles. There was no sense of flow: A set of stairs abutted a bank, so if you ollied down the stairs, you'd run into the bank, and if you rode down the bank, you'd slam into the stairs. The ledges were six inches high instead of the standard two feet. And there was a bizarre, narrow, winding sidewalk with tiny unrideable berms on either side. It felt like the park had been designed by someone who knew nothing about skateboarding, and had been built by whatever sidewalk contractor happened to make the lowest bid.

I rolled around the place for a while, blowing easy tricks, trying to find a zone where I could actually do some real skating. After a while, I just gave up.

Some of the parks-and-recreation officials approached and asked me how I liked their new facility. I didn't to want to hurt anyone's feelings, but I also didn't want to lie. I said, "Honestly? It's pretty bad."

And they said: "You know what? That's what all the local kids have been saying. But we told them, 'Just wait until Tony Hawk gets here. *He'll* show you how to ride it.'"

Because of my failed test flight, they decided to bring in a vert ramp to make sure I'd have something to skate for the big demo the next day. After I was finished, they carted away the ramp and gave the kids their crappy skatepark.

Back home, as I started telling this story to friends, it occurred to me that I was in a position to help stop such foolishness from recurring—to fix the ongoing disconnect between the people in positions to build public skateparks and the kids who ride them.

Skateboarding was going through an upswing in popularity at the time, and this one looked like it would stick. The X Games and my video game had introduced skating to a whole new market: spectators. People who'd never stepped foot on a skateboard were now stopping pros like Bob Burnquist and Andy Macdonald on the street, asking for autographs.

More significantly, young kids were buying skateboards like never before; there were more than 12 million skateboarders in the United States in 2001, but only about 2,000 skateparks. And a lot of those parks were bad—as I'd just learned firsthand outside Chicago.

I also knew that many communities were resistant to building any kind of skatepark. The impoverished ones couldn't afford it. Others were worried about liability. And some feared a skatepark would attract too many punks.

But here's the thing: Kids are going to skate whether or not civic leaders create a place for them to do it. So they end up skating in spots that city officials or school administrators or local business owners have deemed off-limits. That means youngsters who'd never before been in serious trouble suddenly find themselves getting ticketed or arrested or suspended—simply because they want to pursue a sport that they're passionate about. And once a kid gets on the wrong side of the law, for whatever reason, his world can speed downhill.

Doing the Charitable Thing

At this point, my video game was doing very well, and I was making more money than I'd ever imagined. So I approached my family about the idea of starting a charity to help build public skateparks in low-income areas. Pat thought it was a great idea.

My brother Steve agreed to do the paperwork to get it started, write the grant application, and then work part-time as executive director until it got off the ground. My name was more recognizable than ever at that point, so we decided to call it the Tony Hawk Foundation.

We put together a board that included the three of us, my other sister Lenore, and a trio of people with expertise we needed: Kim Novick, then development director for the Surfrider Foundation, who knew all about charitable fundraising and creating programs; Miki Vuckovich, an old friend and longtime skate-mag editor who had experience lobbying for municipal skateparks; and Pierce Flynn, former executive director of the Surfrider Foundation, who had actually run a nonprofit.

Our first order of business was to craft a mission statement. This was what we came up with: "The Tony Hawk Foundation seeks to foster lasting improvements in society, with an emphasis on helping children. Through grants and other charitable donations, the Foundation supports programs focusing on the creation of public skateboard parks, and other causes. The Foundation favors programs that clearly demonstrate that funds received will produce tangible, ongoing, positive results."

In late 2001, I wrote a check for $50,000 to kickstart the foundation. I also promised to donate future appearance fees. Some of my major sponsors

Here I am at the Nathan Lazarus Skatepark grand opening in Nederland, Colorado, named after the 5th grader who helped me win big money on *Are You Smarter Than a 5th Grader?*

From: ▮▮▮▮▮
To: <information@tonyhawk.com>
Subject: r u high

Dear Tony Hawk,

Were you high when you were on, "Are You Smarter Than a 5th Grader?"

at the time (Activision, Heinz Foods for Bagel Bites, ESPN, and Quiksilver) contributed as well.

Shortly after we became an official nonprofit, I got invited to be on a celebrity edition of ABC's hit game show, *Who Wants to Be a Millionaire?* With an assist from Steve as my "phone a friend" lifeline (he's not that smart, just good at googling), I won $125,000 for the foundation. Thanks, Regis. (A few years later, Fox TV asked me to be a contestant on its series *Are You Smarter Than a 5th Grader?*, also for charity. That time I got invaluable help from one of the show's "classmates," an 11-year-old named Nathan, and won $175,000. I was so impressed by Nathan that, in front of the cameras, I promised him we'd help finance a skatepark in his hometown. The park cost about $500,000 total, and we kicked in $75,000. Two years later, I attended the grand opening of the Nathan Lazarus Skatepark in Nederland, Colorado. I stood beside him as he cut the ribbon, then skated for a while in front of a few thousand people. That was a good day. (And it's a good skatepark.)

To get the word out about the foundation, we issued some press releases, and I began to talk about it in interviews and on talk shows. Jaimie Muehlhausen, my company's in-house graphic guru, teamed up with my old friend Ray Underhill to build a website (tonyhawkfoundation.org) so communities could fill out our grant application and read tips on how to develop a community skatepark.

As the first wave of applications poured in, some patterns emerged. A big percentage came from small, impoverished rural communities in the Midwest (particularly Wisconsin, for some mysterious reason). We also got a lot of applications from the West Coast: California, Oregon, and Washington, which all have strong skate scenes.

The West Coast applicants tended to want to build big concrete parks with deep bowls designed primarily for older, experienced skaters. The Midwesterners had cheaper, more modest ambitions. Most were small farming towns seeking to buy prefab obstacles (quarterpipes, fun boxes, pyramids) that they could install on existing flat surfaces. A lot of their proposed parks were the exact same size: 14,400 square feet. It took us a while to figure out that they were converting old, unused tennis courts into skateparks.

The first year we donated to parks, we gave away over $350,000 to 105 projects, with grants ranging from $1,000 to $25,000. The applicants had to be legitimate nonprofits, and they had to be working toward creating a public skatepark in an underprivileged community.

This Ain't No Soccer Field

After the foundation had been up and running for a couple of years, two of our board members took over to run the show. Miki came on as executive director, and Kim stepped up to oversee development and fundraising efforts. Today, the Tony Hawk Foundation has four full-time employees.

In addition to poring over grant applications to determine which projects should receive our money, Miki and his staff have worked to turn the foundation into an invaluable educational resource for anyone grappling with the painful logistics of getting a public skatepark built.

When a skater or parent calls, we tell them how to get their project started and how to push it through the system. When a municipality or local parks-and-recreation administrator calls, we stress the

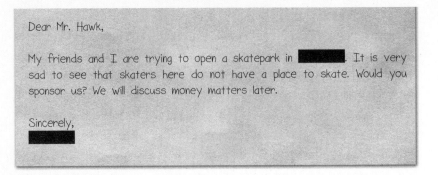

Dear Mr. Hawk,

My friends and I are trying to open a skatepark in ███████. It is very sad to see that skaters here do not have a place to skate. Would you sponsor us? We will discuss money matters later.

Sincerely,

████████

importance of bringing local skateboarders into the process very early, to ensure that they build a park their constituents will actually use.

We remind them that the design decisions that go into building a skatepark are far different from those of such cookie-cutter facilities as basketball courts or soccer fields. No two skateparks are alike. They can be made of concrete, asphalt, wood, steel, or plastic—or some combination thereof. They can range from 1,000 square feet to 100,000 square feet. Too often, bureaucrats heed the advice of reps from a particular line of modular skate obstacles (often made by large playground equipment manufacturers), who sometimes present themselves as unbiased experts but invariably push their own brands.

In 2007, we collaborated with a nonprofit called Skaters for Public Skateparks and the International Association of Skateboard Companies to draft, print, and distribute a 128-page *Public Skatepark Development Guide* (publicskateparkguide.org). It quickly became *the* go-to guide for anyone looking to create a public skatepark. We also field a flood of phone calls and e-mails from skaters and officials who have specific questions, and we've compiled a public database of municipal officials who've succeeded at building skateparks and who are willing to give advice to their peers in the parks-and-recreation world.

At the time this book was written (summer 2010), the foundation has provided technical assistance to some 1,700 communities, and awarded more than $3 million in grants to more than 450 low-income communities in 49 states. (Time to step up, Connecticut.) About 350 of the parks that have received our money are now open, serving around three million skaters annually. Based on those numbers, we figure the foundation has helped to create more than 10 percent of the estimated 3,000 skateparks in the country.

Celebrity Backscratching

One of the keys to the foundation's growth has been our annual "Stand Up for Skateparks" benefit. It's one of those high-end fund-raising events in which well-heeled people pay a few hundred dollars each to eat good food, watch famous performers, and bid on donated auction items. Only ours is far from black tie. It's aimed at kids, and the food is mostly tacos, burgers, hot dogs, and macaroni and cheese. And the entertainment comes in the form of skateboarders and BMXers doing a demo on my vert ramp.

The first one was held in 2004 at a Pinz bowling alley in Los Angeles. The band Blink-182 played, and a bunch of celebrities whom I'd met over the years (Tom Green, David Spade, and Jon Favreau, among others) showed up. We grossed more than $700,000 that year. More important, we planted seeds for future events.

Turns out that one of the richest guys in Southern California, grocery chain magnate Ron Burkle, has a son who loves skateboarding, and after the first event Ron graciously invited us to use his 14-acre estate in Beverly Hills for the next fundraiser. Word got out that our first one had been very kid-friendly, with lots of giveaways (free skate shoes, free backpacks, video games, and toys), and we drew the attention of several celebrities with kids who skate. People like Sean Penn, Jamie Lee Curtis, Lisa Kudrow, Kathy Ireland, and Chuck Liddell (shredordie.com/video/tony-hawk-ride-presents-stand) lent their names to the event and donated generously. We realized we had a fundraising hit on our hands.

In 2008, we decided to hold a secondary event in the Hamptons, in New York, introducing a whole new crowd to California-style fundraising. That one didn't raise as much money as we had hoped, so in 2009 we moved the secondary event to Las Vegas, where it did very well and where we'll keep it for the foreseeable future.

But the primary event will remain in Beverly Hills. We've drawn some cool celebrities over the years, including Lance Armstrong, Andre Agassi, Benicio del Toro, Pamela Anderson, Johnny Knoxville, Travis Barker, Mia Hamm, Howie Mandel, Leeza Gibbons, Sean "Diddy" Combs, Fred Durst, Jakob Dylan, Flea (of the Red Hot Chili Peppers), John Fogerty, Kenny G, Arsenio Hall, Ed Helms, Anthony Kiedis, Dylan Bruno, Stefan Lessard, B. J. Novak, Trent Reznor, Russell Simmons, and Victoria Beckham. In addition to Blink-182, we've had musical performances by Perry Farrell, Social Distortion, and Rancid.

The annual Stand Up for Skateparks fundraiser has turned out to be the foundation's greatest single source of revenue. In recent years, we've added a live "pledge drive" format, in which guests are asked to donate money to a specific skatepark project in an especially needy area. At the 2007 event, over the course of about 15 minutes we raised $80,000 for a park in Compton, the notoriously gang-infested city near Los Angeles. Since then, we've also held live pledge drives for parks in New York City, San Diego, Las Vegas, and Watts.

Meanwhile, over the past decade or so, I've been invited to several fundraisers organized by other sports celebrities, including Muhammad Ali and Andre Agassi. The Agassi event is *the* big sports-celebrity charity gala of the year. It's held in an arena in Vegas, where Agassi grew up, and the performing musicians have included such huge names as Celine Dion and Reba McEntire. Andre is an amazing philanthropist who has single-handedly financed a school for troubled kids in his hometown. At his event, I agreed to donate a free private skate performance and a tour of my office (and lunch) for 10 people. I was stunned when two separate people bid $50,000 for that package, for a total of $100,000...just to see me skate!

In return, Andre donated a private tennis lesson at one of my events, which brought in $10,000 for the Tony Hawk Foundation. You might notice that my donation earned more for his foundation than his did for mine. But don't get any ideas. It's not that people are willing to pay more to see Tony Hawk skate than they are to learn how to hit a tennis ball as hard as Andre Agassi does. It's just that his event attracts a richer crowd.

Clearly, I need to poach his guest list.

Flipping Flapjacks and Mowing Lawns

We select our grant recipients based not only on financial need, but also on how much evidence they provide that the local community is coming together to support the skatepark project. That's actually become a key factor: Have residents, especially local skaters, rallied around the project? It's also become one of my favorite things about the foundation, and about skateparks in general.

The foundation's true mission, it turns out, goes beyond simply giving skateboarders a curvy place to play. We've discovered that the benefits that derive from the process of getting a skatepark built, while not tangible or quantifiable, can be just as valuable as the product itself. If it's done right, a skatepark project can teach young people a lifelong lesson in the power of perseverance, and remind adults that kids with funny haircuts and pierced lips not only can be good people, but also can get things done.

Despite all of the mainstream credibility that skateboarding has received in recent years, many adults still regard skaters as disrespectful troublemakers. Business owners chase them away. City officials pass ordinances to impede them. Police give them tickets. Stigmatized as outsiders, many skateboarders grow up feeling disenfranchised, and the institutionalized image of skaters as delinquents becomes a self-fulfilling prophecy.

In a lot of towns, though, a skatepark—and the effort that goes into getting one built—has proven to be the perfect hammer to break that cycle. At its best, it works like this: A skater gets in trouble (maybe a ticket, maybe a call home from the principal) and complains to his mom and dad that he has no place to skate. His parents persuade him to write a letter to City Hall, or to attend a city council meeting. The kid gets some friends together, puts on his cleanest shirt, sits through a boring meeting, and then makes a nervous but respectful plea for a skatepark. City officials, impressed by the courteous request, decide that it's a good idea and order their parks-and-recreation staff to look into it. The city agrees to donate land for the skatepark but requires the skaters to find the money to build it.

With the help of one or two city officials and a handful of parents, the kids form a committee and spend the next year or two raising money and community awareness. They apply for grants. They hold car washes, barbecues, raffles, and skate-a-thons. They do yard work for their neighbors and donate the wages to the skatepark fund. Eventually, the whole town rallies behind the determined youth brigade. The police chief writes an editorial in the local newspaper praising the kids for their efforts. The local Lions Club holds a pancake breakfast, and the hometown newspaper runs a photo of some beribboned World War II vet flipping flapjacks for skaters.

This is when attitudes change. The kids realize that the adults really want to help them, and the adults realize that the kids are willing to work hard for this thing they love. Most important, the kids discover that they can actually accomplish something by working within the system rather than beating their heads against it or sitting at home complaining about it. They learn how to communicate in a way that will encourage adults to listen, and they go from feeling alienated to empowered.

I don't want to sound sappy, but I'm convinced that when teenagers, parents, police, politicians, business leaders, and civic groups all get together and push the same wheel, and that wheel actually turns, the effort alone makes the world a slightly better place.

Not to mention that the kids end up with a place to skate.

ACKNOWLEDGMENTS

Lhotse Hawk
Riley Hawk
Spencer Hawk
Keegan Hawk
Kadence Hawk
Frank Hawk
Nancy Hawk
Lenore Dale
Pat Hawk
Steve Hawk

Alan Deremo
Pamm Higgins
Dick Dale
Greg Dale
John Dale
Hagen Deremo
Emily Deremo
Will Hawk
Cameron Hawk

■ ■ ■

Ray Underhill
Kerry, Keaton & Olivia
The Mortimer family
Greg Smith
Catherine O
Matt Goodman
Barry Z

Maximillion Cooper
Julie Brangstrup
Jackass crew
Christian Jacobs
Cindy Dunbar
Trent Reznor
Rob Sheridan

■ ■ ■

Jaimie Muehlhausen
Seth Venezia
Jared Prindle
Sandy Dusablon

Shaun Anderson
Steven Perelman
Kevin Staab
Mike "Rooftop" Escamilla

Kim Novick
Miki Vuckovich
CC Flashman
Kirsten Kuhn
Irene Navarro
Angela Rhodehamel

Matt Haring
Derek Richardson
Steve Haring
Ralph D'Amato
Jesse Fritsch
Kris Sale

■ ■ ■

Jim Guerinot
Larry Tull

Lisa Kidd

■ ■ ■

Sarah Hall

Daniel Burch

■ ■ ■

Lisa Shotland
Lowell Taub
Michael Yanover
Lloyd Frischer
Maggie Dumais
Brian Dubin
Andrew Muser
Eric Zohn

Peter Hess
Richard Charnoff
Marc Geiger
June Horton
Amy Flax
Ron Opaleski
David Schwab
Krista Parkinson

■ ■ ■

Bobby Kotick
Will Kassoy
Joanne Wong
Antonio Ramos

Ryh-Ming Poon
Mike Fulkerson
Kathy Vrabeck
Ron Dornink

Yale Miller
Hjalmar Hedman
Lisa Hudson
Dave Pokress
Jeff Kaltreider

Scott Pease
Joel Jewitt
Josh Tsui
Kehau Rodenhurst
Dave Stohl

■ ■ ■

Bob McKnight
Danny Kwock
Russell Nadel
Greg Macias
Greg Perlot
Guy Channin
Josh Katz

Marty Samuels
Mathieu Darrigrand
Matt Ramirez
Mike Matey
Nicolas Foulet
Steve Tully
Bill Bussiere

■ ■ ■

Alex Chalmers
Andy Jones
Andy Macdonald
Bam Margera
Bob Burnquist
Brian Deegan
Brian Sumner
Bucky Lasek
Carey Hart
Chad Kagy
Clifford Adoptante
Colin McKay
Daewon Song
Dave Mirra
David Loy
Dennis McCoy

Derek "Ghost" Burdette
Derek Burlew
Donny Barley
Drake McElroy
Dustin Miller
Elliot Sloan
Eric Koston
Graham Gustin
Greg Garrison
Jamie Bestwick
Jason Ellis
Jean Postec
Jeremy "Twitch" Stenberg
Jeremy Klein
John Parker
Kerry Getz

Kevin Robinson
Kris Markovich
Lance Mountain
Lincoln Ueda
Lyn-Z Adams Hawkins
Mat Hoffman
Matt Ball
Matt Beach
Matt Buyten
Micky Dymond
Mike Cinqmars
Mike Escamilla
Mike Mason
Mike McGill
Mike Vallely
Neal Hendrix
Ocean Howell
Paul Zitzer
Randy Ploesser
Rick Thorne

Rodney Mullen
Ronnie Faisst
Rune Glifberg
Ryan Scheckler
Scott Taylor
Sean Eaton
Sean Nielson
Sergie Ventura
Shaun Gregoire
Shaun Stulz
Shaun White
Shawn Hale
Simon Tabron
Stacy Peralta
Steve Berra
Steve Caballero
Steve Nesser
Todd Richards
Tom Stober
Willy Santos

■ ■ ■

Alex Macleod
Bill Silva
Bruce Haynes
Bruno Musso
Carl Harris
Craig Sneiderman
Dave Seoane
David "Gurn" Kaniski
Ed O'Leary
Ian Voterri
Jill Berliner

Jim Reeder
Jody Morris
Josh Smith
Lowell McGregor
Mike McGinley
Mike Relm
Nick Jeen
Peter Harper
Pierce Flynn
Ray Woodbury
Ryan Young

Shelby Meade
Sound Image

Suzy Shortt
Terry Hardy

■ ■ ■

DJ Aero
Devo
CKY
Social Distortion
Rancid
The Offspring
blink 182
Good Charlotte

Anarchy Orchestra
Pharrell
Me First and the Gimme Gimme's
Pennywise
Perry Ferrell
Jon Goemann
Bruce Haynes

■ ■ ■

Jared Levine
Jeff Endlich
Alex Kohner
Bill Finkelstein
Bob Kahan
Cindy Comito
Corinne Farley
Doug Freeman

Gary Iskowitz
Joe O'Hara
John Sommer
Steve Hassan
Teri Palma
Lisa Ferguson
Sheri Thomas

■ ■ ■

Ron Burkle
Dana White
Chuck Liddell
Tom Greene
David Spade
Jon Favreau
Jaimie Lee Curtis
Lance Armstrong
Chris "BIg black" Boykin

Jack Black
Jon Bon Jovi
Andre Agassi
Mia Hamm
Verne Troyer
Leeza Gibbons
Michael Rappaport
Benecio Del Toro
Kathy Ireland

■ ■ ■

Atiba Jefferson

Chris Miller

Dave Swift

Don and Daniel Bostick

Frank Barbara

Gary Arnold

Noah McMahon

Jessica Barnes

Grant Brittain

Jay Novak

Jeff Taylor

Jeremy Fox

Jeremy Klein

John Schoenfeld

Jose Gomez

Kemp Curley

Mark Dufilho

Morgan Stone

Per Welinder

Tami Kubota

Tom Lochtefeld

Peggy Eskanasi

Dawn Matson

Jessica Hearl

Sarah Liebman

Tait Towers

Tony P

Ron Semiao

Jack Wienart

Chris Steipock

David Hill

CJ Olivares

Jake Munsey

Shon Tomlin

Casey Jenkins

Mike Belcher

Scott Floyd

Bruce Mackenzie

Rob Sumner

Josh Wollock

Bob Ruhland

Walter Lockhart

Jennifer Tabaczuk

Ben Burden Smith

John Lewicki

Kent Voetberg

Vince Thompson

Michael La Kier

Chris Amoroso

Adam Unger

Stacee Sobin

Jeffery Franco

Anthony Vittone

Mitch Galbraith

Dick Glover

Roy Jones

Dave Castrucci

John Bisques

Mark Kvamme

Candi Whitsel

Shannan Valette

Dave Melendez

Marc Joines

Mark Heinken

Joe Bowers

Reggie Barnes

Eric Krantz

Ross Tannenbaum

Terry Sarria
Rey Acevedo
Jerry Dikowitz
Chad DiNenna
Mike Fulkerson
Scott Greenstein
Will Pendarvis
Steve Blatter
Mike Antinoro
Mark Shapiro
Nikki Donofrio
David McKillips
Craig Sims
Noah McKeirnan
Steve James

Craig Drobis
Heather Kindseth
Michael Dahl
John Frame
Matthew Holt
Dan Ambrosio
Sophie Matson
Jadyn Rosario
Frederic Libbrecht
Britt Lyman
Rose Meza
Jim Reeder
Robert Melville
Curtis Ziak

INDEX